A Key to Better Reading

Books by Paul D. Leedy

A KEY TO BETTER READING

THE WONDERFUL WORLD OF BOOKS

READING IMPROVEMENT FOR ADULTS

IMPROVE YOUR READING

READ WITH SPEED AND PRECISION

PERSPECTIVES IN READING:

COLLEGE-ADULT READING INSTRUCTION

A Key to Better Reading

by Paul D. Leedy

McGraw-Hill Book Company / New York Toronto London Sydney

Acknowledgment is made to the following sources for permission to quote from material already published:

Near Vision Test Card by Arthur Hail Keeney, M.D., and Hugh Lyle Duerson, Jr. Copyright © 1958 by the Guild of Prescription Opticians of America, Inc. Reprinted by permission.

"Astigmatism" Ad reprinted by permission of The Better Vision Institute.

If Things Look Bad Now, Think What They Once Were ("Are College Riots Some-thing New?"). Reprinted by permission of the editors of *Dickinson Today*, Dickinson College.

The Art of Problem Solving by Edward Hodnett. Copyright © 1955 by Harper and Brothers. Reprinted by permission of Harper & Row, Publishers, Inc.

Code of Ethics of the International Reading Association reprinted by permission of the International Reading Association.

The article on the *Viking Princess* fire, "Luxury Liner Burns," reprinted by courtesy of The Associated Press and *The* (Washington, D.C.) *Evening Star.*

Monthly Letter reprinted by courtesy of The Royal Bank of Canada.

Editorial from *The New York Times* of October 7, 1962, Section E, page 8, "Autumn Cargoes." Copyright © 1962 by The New York Times Company. Reprinted by permission.

Collage from the business pages of *The New York Times* of September 24 and 27, 1967. Copyright © by The New York Times Company. Reprinted by permission.

What's the Good Word? by Maxwell Nurnberg. Copyright © 1942, 1950 by Maxwell Nurnberg. Reprinted by permission of the author.

Punctuation Pointers by Maxwell Nurnberg. Copyright © 1968 by Maxwell Nurnberg. Reprinted by permission of the author.

The chart from *The 14 Words That Make All the Difference* by Leonard A. Stevens, prepared by Dr. James I. Brown, which appeared in the August, 1956, issue of *Coronet* Magazine, reprinted by permission of Collins-Knowlton-Wing, Inc.

246653

Before you go further—read this...

Do you read like an adult?

Do you tackle a page of print with that consummate competence, that complete mastery which can extract the meaning from the page with least effort and greatest efficiency?

Few people do. In large majority, adults as readers are immature. Shackled by inadequate reading habits learned principally in childhood, our grade school skills produce low-yield results when compared with the total effort and investment of time that most adults devote to reading.

This is all the more disturbing in the light of the demands that reading makes upon each of our lives. With the occupational requirements for reading, the need to study, and the pressures to keep abreast of events becoming increasingly demanding, there is greater need than ever to read like an adult.

Although this book is expressly addressed to the so-called "adult audience," teen-agers might profit equally well from its contents. For, it is during adolescence that the foundations should be firmly laid for those reading habits and skills that will ever afterward make mature and masterful readers.

Many of the techniques, in fact, that lead to maturity in reading ought to be acquired early and practiced actively throughout an entire lifetime. The disquieting fact is that so much that an adult needs to know in order to read like an adult is seldom specifically taught in school. All too often, *instruction* in reading ceases in the intermediate grades; and, from then on throughout the rest of his life, the individual hobbles along the avenues of print with grossly inadequate reading skills which, if they were learned at all, were learned only in the lower grades. Little wonder, then, that nearly every adult openly admits his inability to read well. He lacks the know-how, the adroitness, the skill to maneuver in the realm of the printed word. And today's world demands that every adult be able to do so.

Many suggestions have been proposed to provide a solution for the adult's problem. Many books have been written purporting to give him the key to the secrets of reading the printed word.

"Speed" reading has recently become a fad. It is also a fallacy. For, if you are to read like an adult, you need much more than mere speed. If you are to absorb the page in record time, you must do more than engage in headlong flight. Rather, you must understand the intricate behavior of thought in print. This involves more than merely scurrying down the page or seeing facts in rapid succession and attempting to remember them. Real reading instruction incorporates into the total approach all that research, scholarship, and years of experience dictate as the best ways to teach an adult to read.

One of the outstanding characteristics of the mature reader is that he thinks *as* he reads: he anticipates; he evaluates; and he keeps oriented always to the thought that is being expressed, to the words that are being employed, and to the inferences and interpretations arising out of both of these. Mature reading is, thus, a complex intellectual process, and much that is called "reading" goes on in the mind of the reader. To read is to think. Consequently, the adult reader does several things at one time while "reading." He is aware of the role of the author, the power and suggestive force of the word, and the efficiency of the proper reading technique, which when used adroitly, like a precise tool for a particular job, helps him to cull the meaning quickly and fully from the printed page.

In approach, this book is essentially simple. It begins with what the average reader needs to know in order to read well —to read like an adult. It begins at the point where, in the public schools, the reading instruction of most adult readers ceased. It tells in simple language exactly how thought is incorporated and how it behaves in print.

There is no wasted motion in this book in the form of dull exercises intended to accelerate speed and improve comprehension. At best, these are artificial devices and may be very unrealistic in measuring objectively those elusive factors of "speed" and "comprehension." Instead, the book is devoted to practical suggestions for reading improvement. It offers you a program that you can put into practice immediately. You do not have to spend weeks or months of "tooling up" for better reading—hours of valuable time working on eye movements or disciplining the extraocular musculature. Rather, the book is aimed directly at the immediate needs of the modern adult: such basic matters as reading the newspaper, reducing the pile on the office desk, and handling effectively subtle propaganda and sales talk. And, just for those who have some leisure time, a closing chapter is devoted to reading for reading's sake. There are also built-in aids to make the improvement of your reading less of a task and more of a pleasure.

Every book holds within it the inestimable contributions of others. Those to whom I am most deeply and graciously indebted in this volume are the countless adults who comprised my classes in reading improvement during the many years when I was senior specialist and chief consultant in college and adult reading at The Reading Institute, New York University; the many groups of executives and professional personnel in some of the large corporations and financial institutions in New York City whom I have assisted in reducing the pile on the office desk; and those Congressmen who have composed my classes at The Graduate School, Department of Agriculture, Washington, D.C. To all these men and women, wherever they may be, I acknowledge a sincere and abiding debt of gratitude. I deeply appreciate also the courtesy of Mr. John Heron, of the Royal Bank of Canada, who generously gave permission to reprint his excellent advice on "Building a Home Library," which originally appeared as a Royal Bank of Canada, *Monthly Letter.* Further, I appreciate the very kind generosity of Dr. Maxwell Nurnberg, who has granted full permission to use some of the material from his newest book, *Punctuation Pointers*—a book which is racing with mine for first appearance from the press.

Finally, in the making of books, wives are utterly indispensable. Without them no book would ever come to press. In that respect this book is no exception. And so, I conclude with a low bow and a flourish of trumpets for the help afforded me by the first lady of these pages.

Paul D. Leedy

Washington, D.C.
August 22, 1966

Contents

A Key to Better Reading

1. Do you have what it takes to read well?

Good reading depends on you.

It depends on how alert you are, how logically you think, how clearly you follow the thought of another, how well you remember, how extensive your knowledge is, and how great your facility is in the use of words.

It depends on other factors also: on your eyes and what they do; on your emotions, your prejudices; and on your ability to separate the essential from the peripheral, the required from the incidental, the main issue from the details. Good reading demands that you be alive, aware and alert, to every meaning, every nuance, every implication of the printed word.

There is no magic formula for better reading.

Effective reading is much more than merely ogling your eyes across a line of print, or attempting to see more at a single glance, or sweeping your eyes down the center of the page in an effort to scoop up ideas.

Effective reading is a fully aware and agile mind in contact with the printed word. It takes an understanding of the ways of print to be able to negotiate your way quickly and effortlessly through a maze of words. It requires those skills and abilities which every effective reader possesses: a knowledge of the manner in which thought is presented through the magic of the printed word. There is a logic and a rationale of communication, as there is a logic and a rationale to all the other activities of our daily lives. At the very outset of your approach to reading improvement, you should fully appreciate that words do behave on the page according to certain principles of communication and laws of language. The effective reader understands how these operate. In the pages ahead we shall discuss these principles and show how they may be utilized in improving your skill with the printed page and increasing your reading power.

Any reader can become a better reader.

But if you aim to improve, you will soon find that the onus of responsibility is squarely upon you. To read better will require practice on your part, and a little time set aside regularly each day—either in bulk or at odd moments—will reward you more than an enthusiastic beginning that fizzles before it gets under way. As with other skills, you will perhaps learn slowly at first, but then you will acquire proficiency with greater and greater acceleration until you will see yourself making real strides toward better reading.

Some of the skills that will improve your reading need not be practiced only in the presence of the printed page. You can improve your proficiency in some of these skills while driving to the office, waiting for a bus, expecting a phone call, or riding home on the train. Every golfer has learned that he does not always need to be on the putting green to practice his stroke. You, likewise, can begin at once to shore up some of your fundamental habits that will contribute to better reading—and, incidentally, you will find that by doing so you will also increase your total efficiency.

You must continue, however, to work at improving these personal qualities as you learn the secrets and the strategy for the conquest of the realm of print. By so doing, you will before long be reading better and, ultimately, you will slowly become aware that you are a better reader and generally a more knowledgeable person.

The requirements are simple.

Anyone with normal intelligence can learn to develop the skill of reading rapidly, with satisfactory comprehension, and with critical insight; and effective reading demands all *three* of these emphases.

Effective reading

Speed alone, without the other components of effective reading, may be mere reckless and meaningless haste and, by itself, has little virtue. Comprehension without speed can be a slow ordeal of drudgery shackling you to the page, wearing you down because of your slowness of pace, and hindering that fleetness of mind without which the subtler overtones of the author's thought are usually lost. Both speed and comprehension, without insight and critical evaluation, may perhaps make you a glittering performer with the printed page without your ever sensing what it means to read really well.

This chapter, therefore, will talk about those personal qualities and fundamental habits without which you cannot read up to your maximum potential. The chapter will be in the nature of a personal inventory, an opportunity for self-examination, a chance to appraise what assets you already have and those you need to develop in order to be a really powerful and effective master of the printed page.

Francis Bacon declared, "Reading maketh a full man." He might with equal truth have said, "Reading demandeth the entire man." For in a very real sense the demands of effective reading call at one time or another on those habits and abilities that make the whole man. The demands which a page of print make upon the reader are varied and, if he is to read well, require a broad spectrum of many aptitudes, abilities, and habits of thought.

Let us see what some of these qualities are.

Alertness

Every top-flight reader is alert. He is sensitive to many features of the page which the less expert reader passes over with apathetic nonchalance. Insensitivity to style, to word, to structure, to thought—this is one of the first signs of immaturity in reading.

Good reading, on the other hand, demands that the mind confronting the page be wide awake. Active contact with the word, the phrase, the thought which the author is seeking to develop demands that the mind of the reader be working: inquiring, observing, concentrating, paying attention to what the author is saying and has said, and following closely his argument or explanation as it progresses logically from point to point.

Alertness in reading connotes exactly what the word originally meant. Of Italian origin, it was a term that signified "standing upon a watchtower or rampart of the city and being constantly on the *qui vive*." That is precisely what every good reader does. He occupies a vantage point with respect to the words of the author, regarding them with vigilant scrutiny, being always on the lookout for whatever the author may say or suggest. Not a comma nor a colon gets by his eye unnoticed; he is sensitive to the shade and suggestion of a word.

Edward L. Thorndike, almost half a century ago, described reading as thinking. What he meant was that no effective reader ever regards reading as a merely passive activity.

Don't just sit there, waiting to see what the page will say to you. Participate. Reading is an all-energy engagement, a completely captivating activity. When you read, read!

Reading ought to be a high-intensity spark.

For many it is a low, smouldering fire, through the smoke and haze of which they comprehend poorly. They begin a paragraph, and before they have read three or four sentences they are merely letting words drift before their eyes; and by the middle of the paragraph such readers are not certain as to what the author is saying nor how his words will form that larger verbal structure—the "development" of the main idea.

Pay attention to what the author is saying. Apply your mind to the idea; keep it there until the author exhausts the pursuit of one thought and, with the next paragraph, sets you hot on the trail of another. This is what it means to read with alertness and attention.

Literally, attention means "to stretch the mind." And stretching the mind, and keeping it stretched, is not always either an easy or a comfortable task. Anyone who has observed young children is aware of their inability to keep their attention focused for any considerable length of time. Such brevity of application psychologists describe as "short attention span." The phenomenon is not limited to children. Many adults while reading also have short attention span. They read a main idea in the first sentence of a paragraph; and three sentences later they have no idea at all what the main idea of the paragraph is!

For all who expect to improve their reading, therefore, alertness and attention are basic qualities, the *sine qua non*, in fact, of the effective reader. Like any other habit, the habit of being alert, alive, and attentive as you read develops only by constant application and unremitting practice.

How long has it been since you have checked your ability to be alert, alive, and thinking while you read? Let's see how aware and attentive you really are.

Read the following brief selection in your usual manner and *only once*. After you have finished reading, you will be directed to turn to page 161, where you will find certain questions designed to reveal the degree to which you were alert while reading.

Incidentally, in this test your rate of reading is also important. Check your watch and note the *exact* time you begin reading the selection. Jot the beginning time in the blanks below, at the head of the selection. At the conclusion of your reading this selection you will be asked again to note the precise time and again to jot it down. Read normally. Now, note your time, jot it down, then read:

Beginning time: —— minutes, —— seconds.

Eagerness to solve a problem—or to punch somebody in the nose—before the problem has been properly identified accounts for much of the inefficiency and grief associated with the vast human activity of problem causing. Your first act as a practicing problem solver is to hold everything until you have disentangled your problem from the general problem situation that enfolds and often obscures it.

The office manager in one of the branches of your business tells you that she is thinking of quitting because she is being unfairly overworked. She implies that you are responsible for her troubles. As her boss, in a way you are. But you resent the hostility and the inference that you are indifferent to the welfare of your employees. In short order you could be embroiled in a bootless wrangle. Instead, you try to isolate the specific problem in the general situation! You concede that the manager has too much to do, if he says he has. But you cannot work on that alone? After a while he clarifies the situation as follows: The growth in the volume of business at that branch has increased his load and particularly his personnel duties. He finally identifies his problem more exactly in this way: "Personnel has grown too big for me to handle along with my other work." Your solution is then clear. You give him an assistant to take care of personnel and to help him in other ways.[1]

Finishing time: —— minutes, —— seconds.

Now, turn to page 161 and, without referring back to the selection above, answer the questions.

[1] Adapted from Edward Hodnett, *The Art of Problem Solving*, New York: Harper and Brothers, page 11.

Recall

A good beginning is half the journey, so says the old adage.

And the adage holds a suggestion for reading improvement. When you have begun to be alert, then you have laid the foundation for many other approaches to reading improvement. Perhaps the aptitude which is most necessary for successful comprehension, aside from alertness, is precision of recall or accuracy of memory. Comprehension is an omnibus term. It is really a complex of many factors: attention, recall, critical and structural thinking, and other abilities that we shall discuss later.

One fact, however, is fortunate. You can improve your recall ability. Most of the time we do not work very hard at improving memory or recall power. Furthermore, we are frequently insensitive to our deficiencies and the necessity to do something about them. Then a reading test or the inability to report accurately what we have read nudges us into an awareness that we may not "be sure of the facts," that we have not comprehended very well. These are subtle signs, but they hint at underlying deficiencies which militate against the best in reading comprehension.

Little everyday experiences may also be the telltale signs of the need for better recall ability. Take this instance. You are walking down the street with a friend when suddenly he meets one of his acquaintances to whom he introduces you. "John, meet Ralph Smallwood." You shake hands; and after a brief exchange of the conventional patter of small talk, you discover Smallwood, like yourself, is an avid hiker and mountain climber. You tell him that you frequently go out for a day's excursion in the hills. He suggests, "Why don't we plan to go out with each other sometime? Call me: HIghland 1-4202." You promise that you will call him and prepare to depart. Awkwardly you stammer, "Er—it was good to meet you, Mr.—er . . ." hoping that your new friend will take the cue and supply his name.

Does a situation like that ever happen to you? If so, it's a warning, a sign that you might well recognize and do something about—especially if you are planning to be a better reader. Chances are that you are not remembering the details of what you read any more successfully or accurately than you remembered your new friend's name. Remembering is a skill that can be developed. It grows stronger with the purposeful exercise of it each day.

But how can you improve your memory and increase your accuracy of recall?

Try three steps to greater memory power.

(1) *Resolve to remember.* Good memory, like most other things worth having, is not fortuitous. It begins with a firm resolve to practice the techniques of remembering at every opportunity. The data recalled may be simple and relatively inconsequential. It is not *what* is recalled but the act of recall itself that is important. Like the genie from Aladdin's lamp, it is the appearance of the fact at the instant of your command that is the consummation devoutly to be wished. Think, for example, how much loose data there is lying around in your mind which you have never bothered to summon forth. All of it is valuable for building a dynamic and immediate recall.

What is the middle initial of that business acquaintance whose name you have seen in print so many times? Precisely what is that cousin's address to whom you write occasionally? Do you always need to check your address book to be *sure* you're right? What about phone numbers, house numbers, your own automobile registration number, your social security number? How many of these can you recall accurately and immediately? Do you know your hat size, your shoe size, your waist measure without a recheck? You have just finished a news story. How many facts and figures can you recall exactly? Jot them down; then, compare your accuracy and extent of recollection with the news account itself. How many yards in a mile? inches in a meter? pounds in a long ton? Such trivia are not trivia, but: the raw material of recall power.

Better reading begins with better comprehension; better comprehension begins with improving your accuracy of recall.

(2) *Rescue the fact frequently.* Facts do not vanish from the mind in a flash. Rather, they sink slowly from awareness to oblivion like victims in a quicksand. They can be recalled and rescued if they are sought in time. The more frequently you rescue facts, the easier the rescue operation becomes. In short, you remember better because you do not let what you have heard, or seen, or read sink irretrievably into the quicksands of oblivion.

Opportunities for fact-recall are all about you. What was the license number of the car that passed you just a moment ago? (You may not have noticed. That, perhaps, because you were not alert!) What was the telephone number you just dialed? The name of the person to whom you have just been introduced? These are a few of the hundreds of opportunities that you have each day. Make them fleeting, golden opportunities to strengthen your power of recall. Flash back for facts and you will find that seemingly forgotten data becomes easier and easier to retrieve after an amazingly small amount of practice.

(3) *Find a formula.* Ingenuity can boost your recall ability to new heights. Make the most of your inventiveness and imagination. Put these resources to work in helping you to remember what you have read. Here is an example: you are reading Fred Hoyle on the structure of the galaxy and the temperatures of the stars. Each star, you learn, belongs to a particular temperature class, and these temperature categories

are arbitrarily designated by certain letters of the alphabet. From the hottest to the coolest stars, the classes are as follows: O, B, A, F, G, K, M, R, N, S.

Suppose for some reason you wish to remember that sequence of stellar temperature classifications. How would you remember that letter series and *never* forget it? Use your imagination. Astronomy students have used theirs and here's what they have come up with: *O*h, *Be* *A* *F*ine *G*irl; *K*iss *M*e *R*ight *N*ow, *S*weetheart!

Now, forget that red-hot series if you can!

Already in this chapter you have had an opportunity to remember data by means of a formula. Were you alert? Ingenious?

Let's check your recall ability. Turn to page 162. There you will find a group of simple questions on the material which you have just read in this section on Recall. Answer the questions without referring to this section.

Vision and Perception

Reading is a visual process. It demands certain visual skills and abilities, some of which are subject to conscious improvement; others, like pulse rate or respiration, are largely subconscious. Much has been written about the function of the eyes in reading—eye movements, eye span, the development of an ever-wider perceptual grasp. These are professional and technical aspects of reading which have been the subject of considerable research and discussion. Eye movements, as such, are a physiological function and, like many similar functions of the human body, are automatic and function best, perhaps, when the reader does not think too much about them.

Eye movements are more symptomatic of poor reading performance than the cause of it. Excessive fixations or regressions may retard the reader, but they are not basically matters of the eye but of the mind.

The eyes while reading generally take care of themselves.

Reading is essentially a brain process, and its excellence or inferiority depends on many aspects of the individual. The whole nervous system is involved—especially your emotional reactions and the logic of your thinking. The eye itself is merely an instrument of vision.

Contrary to much popular opinion, better reading does not depend upon a mere forcing of the eyes to move ever more rapidly down the lanes of print. The fleetness of the eyes lies in the ability of the brain to absorb, assimilate, and to associate ideas which are resident in the words which the eyes perceive. Until the brain is nimble, the eyes are sluggish.

Reading, therefore, depends on many additional factors other than those of vision, perception span, and speed of eye movements. It depends, among other things, on the fullness of your vocabulary resources, on your background knowledge, and on your general education. The more you know, the better you read. For most readers the extraocular musculature of the eye will be quite agile enough to pace the eyes across the page. Efficient reading does not begin here; it lies much deeper, in the more vital and complex areas of the brain.

But do not underestimate the importance of vision. Correct vision is critical to effective reading. Like many deficiencies to which we become so accustomed that we are not aware of having them, visual disability may hinder effective reading without the reader sensing that his eyes are not functioning at their optimal potential. Middle-aged adults, especially, need to be alert to any diminution of visual acuity, especially when reading at near point—that is, with the reading matter 15 to 18 inches from the eyes.

Depending upon the individual, the "vicinity of the forties" may be a time of transition. At this time in life, the tiny ciliary muscles that control the accommodation of the crystalline lens of the eye to near- and far-point seeing lose their tonicity. The onset of the malfunction may be subtle, and a person who has had otherwise excellent vision throughout his lifetime may not at first be aware of the change that is taking place. *Presbyopia* is the medical term which describes this condition. The individual becomes more and more far-sighted. He pushes the page away in order to see the print more clearly. This is the time in a person's life when, if he has previously been wearing glasses, the ophthalmologist usually prescribes bifocal lenses: one segment to be used in distance seeing, the other segment for reading. Sometimes, where there are no other complicating factors, such as astigmatism or a phoria,[2] a person needs only one set of lenses, and these he frequently calls his "reading glasses."

Your eyes are your most precious possession. They should have the professional care of an ophthalmologist or an optometrist. An ophthalmologist is a physician who has done his internship in ophthalmology and who specializes in the pathology and treatment of the diseases of the eye. He has an M.D. degree. The optometrist, a Doctor of Optometry (O.D.), is a specialist in vision and visual care. He does not treat eye disease, nor does he use or prescribe medication of any sort. Upon detection and recognition of the presence of disease in the eye, he refers the patient for other specialized professional care. Since the eye is a part of a larger functioning organism, other conditions such as diabetes, arteriosclerosis, hypertension, or similar pathological situations may contribute to visual disability. In such instances, the services of an ophthalmologist would be indicated. An optician, as distinguished from the foregoing specialists, is one who makes, fits, or deals in optical glasses or instruments, and has no license to diagnose or prescribe for visual defects.

Certain simple screening tests and inventories may reveal the need for expert, professional care. Some of these you will find in the test section on page 163. Turn to this page and see how well you do with these crude attempts to assess your

[2] *Phoria* is a technical term meaning muscular imbalance. There are several kinds, any one of which we call "a phoria."

visual status. Remember, these tests are superficial and un-professional and are intended to provide you with only a gross indication of your visual condition. If they seem to indicate any difficulty with your vision, you should of course seek competent professional care.

Seeing and reading should be a comfortable, effortless ac-complishment. Anything which deviates from this should alert the reader that something may be wrong and that profes-sional help may be necessary.

What, then, happens when we read? The eyes move across the line of print, not in continuous sweeps, but in little jerks, called *saccades* or *saccadic movements*. During the forward motion, the eyes see very little if anything at all. When they pause to scan the words—such pauses are called *fixations*—then the eyes really see. This sight data is then relayed by means of the optic nerve to the brain, where, in an amazing, complex, data-decoding process, the visual impressions of the words that were originally on the page are converted from neurological impulses into thought and meaning. As soon as the mind grasps the meaning, the eyes are then commanded by the brain to move forward, which they do, scooping up another "eyeful." The mere seeing of the word is not reading; it is nothing more than visual perception. The perceptive process sets up a neural impulse in the cells of the retina, which impulses, "telegraphed" to the brain, become the data for reading.

Background information and experience figure heavily in reading proficiently. Terms which may be meaningless to the average person assume a significance and meaning to a per-son whose experience or knowledge equips him to recognize them as precise expressions of a specific concept. When this happens, we read. For example, to the average person a "tun-nel diode" may mean nothing at all—or he may get the idea that it is an electronic component that is used in subter-ranean passages. But when an electronic engineer sees these words, he "reads" them as "a type of single p-n junction device which has obtained its name from the fact that its operation depends upon a physical phenomenon, known as quantum-mechanical tunneling."

And even with these words of explanation, the average person may still be as much in the dark and as bewildered as ever. Does it mean that his eyes or his eye movements are at fault? No. Does it mean that he cannot read the phrase "tunnel diode"? Yes. Even the explanation of the term he may read poorly, in that he may but dimly comprehend really what the term means. For those who don't know what a "single p-n junction device" or "quantum-mechanical tunneling" is, these particular fixations are meaningless, regardless of how slowly or quickly they may be perceived. Herein lies the fallacy of the suggestion that the faster the eyes move across the page, the faster we read. We read only as fast as the brain converts the verbal perception into meaning.

Speed and comprehension of reading may, however, be improved through visual alertness. Perhaps one of the wisest observations ever made is: "Eyes they have and they see not." These words are especially appropriate with respect to reading. Whether it is a page of print or an everyday occurrence, most people are not observant. They simply do not see what is to be seen. Perception is a skill, and it can be improved with constant use and determination. It is one of the keys to speed and comprehension in reading.

All kinds of devices are used in professional reading centers to improve perceptual acuity. The flashmeter, or tachistoscope, presents data in split-second intervals as a challenge to the reader's grasping power. Reading films are also used. In these, the words of reading selections are flashed across the screen in larger and larger units at more and more rapid intervals as a challenge to read faster. The controlled reader is another device for flashing data in much the same way.

All these devices have one aim: to present data and to snatch it away in a brief instant of time so that the reader will sharpen his speed of perception—his skill at grasping the fleeting fact at a glance. But you do not need expensive equipment or the trained services of a reading center to provide you with opportunities for improving your perceptual skills. Each day offers you innumerable opportunities to improve.

As you are riding in a train or bus, try to read the road and shop signs that flash by your line of vision. See if with repeated trials you cannot grasp more and more. After each television hour, the list of "credits" is reeled from the bottom to the top of the TV screen. How agile are you at reading the entire list? Practice on it after each show. Stand on any corner and watch the automobiles flash past. Can you read the registration tags accurately? Take a note pad, jot them down. Flex the pages of a book. Let the pages slip in a continuous succession from under your thumb. Aim for a half-second exposure of each page. Try to see as much of the material on the page as possible, by glance absorption. When you have finished flexing the pages with your left hand, reverse the process using your right hand. Twice through the book this way should give you a fairly accurate impression of the contents, the format, the style of the volume. When you have finished, tell yourself as much as possible about the contents of the volume—or better yet, write it down.

Let's see how perceptive you are right now.

Read this sentence:

> FINISHED FILES ARE THE RE-
> SULT OF YEARS OF SCIEN-
> TIFIC STUDY COMBINED WITH
> THE EXPERIENCE OF YEARS.

Now count the F's in that sentence. Count them *only once;*

do not go back and count them again. How many F's did you find? Enter the number here: ___ . Now turn to the Answer Key, on page 187, to find the correct answer and an evaluation of your perceptive level.

Word-Hoard

The Anglo-Saxons had a phrase for it. In an imaginative, vivid flash of primitive genius, they expressed in a phrase the facility with words—the possession of a dynamic vocabulary. They called it one's "word-hoard."

When, for example, any of their heroes had something of importance to say, they expressed that act of utterance dramatically: "The warriors' leader his word-hoard unlocked . . ."

Every superior reader has a hoard of accumulated, powerful words; for the word is the only magic that man has been able to possess. By the magic of words alone, thought passes from mind to mind. Whether printed or spoken or heard, the word is the important thing. The greater word-hoard the reader has, the more effortless, the more powerful his reading will be.

Psychologists have found a high correlation between an extensive vocabulary and a superior I.Q. Word power augurs success. Leaders in business, personnel directors, and others who deal with men and jobs have noted that those who have been most successful are also those at no loss to express their thoughts by means of the precise word. Mental ability and prognosis of success is nearly always in direct ratio to the size of one's word-hoard. The more words you know, the greater facility you have for dealing in ideas, in abstractions, in concepts. These are captured, considered, and criticized by means of the word.

If you are to read well, you should make a conscious effort to enlarge your word-hoard daily. Notice every new word you encounter. Jot it down; look it up, as soon as possible.

Use that word somewhere, somehow, in your writing, in your speaking, in your thinking. Perhaps this last activity may be as important, if not more so, than either of the other two. Familiarity with a word begins by employing it in your own thinking. When it becomes familiar to your thinking, it never sounds strange on your tongue.

Here are some suggestions for increasing your word-hoard. Keep a pack of cards, on one side of which you write the word you wish to learn; on the other side, jot down a brief definition or several synonyms for the word with, perhaps, the basic root meanings from which the word has evolved. Review these cards several times daily at odd moments.

Carry a pocket dictionary with you. Use it to suggest new words, to review old ones. One week go through all the "A" words. Check in the margin the unfamiliar ones. Transfer these to cards. Add them to your word-hoard. Next week the "B" words; and so in twenty-six weeks or less (the J, Q, X, Y, and Z weeks may be somewhat slim) you will have learned every word in the dictionary. January to June would do it easily!

Any adult ought to know *every* word in a small pocket dictionary and have them available for instant use. Why not set this as your first vocabulary goal? After the pocket edition, then tackle the *Webster's Collegiate* the same way. Within a year you'll be amazed at your word-hoard and at the increased power in reading, thinking, and speaking that a dynamic vocabulary can provide.

To help you increase your word resources more easily the chart on the accompanying page may add high octane to the learning process. Dr. James I. Brown, of the University of Minnesota, a leading authority in reading and vocabulary study, made a comprehensive analysis of all the words in the *Webster's Collegiate Dictionary* and tabulated the prefixes (the beginnings of words) and the roots (or basic-meaning elements) in the order of their frequency. The most important prefixes and roots he selected for inclusion in the *Master Chart of 100,000 Words*. The chart dissects fourteen master words into prefixes, in the column to the left, and roots, in the column to the right-of-center, together with variant spellings of each. Learn the various prefixes and roots so that you recognize them instantaneously and know their meanings unmistakably. Work with a dictionary. Note how the present meaning of the word reflects its original meaning contained in its basic elements. In the first master word, for example, *detain* comes from *de-*, meaning "down," and *tain*, "to hold." Literally, "to detain" means to hold one down so that he cannot go further.

Now, here is your key to a supervocabulary: the fourteen basic words.

As you work more and more with words, reflecting upon their original meanings, you will come to appreciate the whole spectrum of overtone and nuance which a word may have; your reading will be more rewarding and your comprehension of the thought more keen and insightful. You will become sensitive to shades of meaning as never before. The printed words will glow with shimmerings of thought which otherwise you would not have realized were there. You will find yourself reading with more appreciation, more comprehension, more understanding of the thought of the author. This is exactly what the best reading should be. All too many readers miss it. For to read is to open a book with expectation, and to lay it down with insight!

How large is your present word-hoard? How precisely do you know the meanings of the words that you read? Turn to page 166 to find out.

Structure Sense

Good readers are invariably aware of the larger structuring of the thought on the page. This is what psychologists might

KEY TO 100,000 WORDS

	PREFIX	ITS OTHER SPELLINGS	ITS MEANING	MASTER WORDS	ROOT	ITS OTHER SPELLINGS	ITS MEANING
1.	DE-	—	Down or Away	**DETAIN**	TAIN	Ten, Tin	To Have or Hold
2.	INTER-	—	Between	**INTERMITTENT**	MITT	Miss, Mis, Mit	To Send
3.	PRE-	—	Before	**PRECEPT**	CEPT	Cap, Capt, Ceiv, Ceit, Cip	To Take or Seize
4.	OB-	Oc- Of- Op-	To, Toward, Against	**OFFER**	FER	Lat, Lay	To Bear or Carry
5.	IN-	Il- Im- Ir-	Into	**INSIST**	SIST	Sta	To Stand, Endure or Persist
6.	MONO-	—	One or Alone	**MONOGRAPH**	GRAPH	—	To Write
7.	EPI-	—	Over, Upon or Beside	**EPILOGUE**	LOG	Ology	Speech or Science
8.	AD-	A- Ac- Ag- Al- An- Ap- Ar- As- At-	To or Towards	**ASPECT**	SPECT	Spec, Spi, Spy	To Look
9.	UN-	—	Not	**UNCOMPLICATED**	PLIC	Play Plex, Ploy, Ply,	To Fold, Bend, Twist or Interweave
	COM-	Co- Col- Con- Cor-	With or Together				
10.	NON-	—	Not	**NONEXTENDED**	TEND	Tens, Tent	To Stretch
	EX-	E- Ef-	Out or Formerly				
11.	RE-	—	Back or Again	**REPRODUCTION**	DUCT	Duc, Duit, Duk	To Lead, Make, Shape or Fashion
	PRO-	—	Forward or In Favor of				
12.	IN-	Il- Im- Ir-	Not	**INDISPOSED**	POS	Pound, Pon, Post	To Put or Place
	DIS-	Di- Dif-	Apart From				
13.	OVER-	—	Above	**OVERSUFFICIENT**	FIC	Fac, Fact, Fash Feat,	To Make or Do
	SUB-	Suc- Suf- Sug- Sup- Sur- Sus-	Under				
14.	MIS-	—	Wrong or Wrongly	**MISTRANSCRIBE**	SCRIBE	Scrip, Scriv	To Write
	TRANS-	Tra- Tran-	Across or Beyond				

call the *gestalt:* the total organization, the larger integrated pattern, the seeing of the whole in terms of its parts.

Authors do not merely write; they present their thoughts in a definite plan of organization which makes their writing coherent and their thought easy to comprehend.

When a cartographer glances at a map, he sees much more than a flatland. He sees the rolling undulations of a countryside, river valleys, and the awesomeness of majestic mountains. Just so, the expert reader sees the towering importance of the main thought masses and the less important lowlands of detail as soon as he glances at a page. All who read with speed and awareness read in this way. The poor reader seldom looks for thought structure or organization, and for him reading is merely the slow plodding through a word jungle: an uncomprehending gaze at a flatland of print.

What kind of reader are you? How sensitive are you to the topography and organization of the thought? Can you stand above the page, looking down upon it, and see the general configuration of the ideas and the logic of their arrangement? Many people cannot understand how complicated machines operate because they do not comprehend the entire train of the mechanism. They fail to see the relationship of the operation of part to part and of all the parts to the operation of the whole. Many readers are like that. They are mere word viewers, page plodders who read isolated sentences, or parts of sentences; and, absorbing a fragment of thought at a time, they fail to comprehend the integral place of these little details in the larger configuration of the main idea, or the constellation of main ideas in the vaster terrain of the thought.

Why not test your own proficiency in sensing the structure and organization of the thought. Turn to page 167.

Increasing Speed of Reading

Reading speed is a by-product of better reading. Your pace will improve when you bring to focus all those qualities which comprise the effective reader. This chapter has discussed those qualities that are basic and essential for better reading and, consequently, for rapid reading.

An alert, versatile mind builds speed as it darts with lightning awareness across or down the page, cutting through unnecessary verbiage in a clean, clear pursuit of the thought. Such a mind examines the page and the writing for significant features and evaluates reading conditions in terms of the ease or difficulty of the style, adjusting its pace accordingly.

A broad and adequate vocabulary likewise assists in increasing speed of reading. When unfamiliar and unknown words stand in the way of the reader they impede his pace and slow his progress. A mind unhampered by unfamiliar words gets there faster and with far greater grasp of the author's thought.

Your speed may also be hampered if your visual performance is poor. Should you be straining to see or looking at lines of printed symbols whose outlines are blurred or indistinct, you cannot read at optimal pace.

But sometimes even with 20/20 vision the eyes need discipline to become more perceptive and alert. You may look and still not see. Then you may need to go back to look again. Such going back to see something twice is called *regression,* and usually results from inattention or failure to perceive as keenly as you might have done the first time the data was presented to your eyes. Any retracing, whether on the road or on the page, means loss of speed and impaired progress.

Finally, speed is aided by looking down on the writing, seeking to see it as a domain of thought unrolled from horizon to horizon. When you see your reading thus you are then able to spot the structural and typographical landmarks on the way ahead. Because you know the direction of the throughway of thought, you can travel it more quickly.

Speed, of course, is relative and varies according to reading conditions. No one will climb the steep hills of difficult thought or roar through the rich and varied landscape of poetry as quickly as he will spin along the easy stretches where the prose is less demanding and easier to comprehend.

In this chapter we have looked at some of the qualities necessary to become a superior reader. In the next chapter we shall consider what the superior reader does with a page of print.

Before leaving this chapter, however, you should have some appraisal of your total strengths and weaknesses. A profile of the factors which comprise reading aptitude would help you to get started on your reading improvement program in a realistic manner. Such a profile is provided on page 169. The directions on page 168, under the section, "And Now Draw Your Profile . . ." will assist you in constructing the diagnostic chart and in discovering your needs. Before you go further, let's see where you now stand.

2. *What to do with a page of print*

Look!

Look at this page.

Hold it away from you—at arm's length. Push it out there as far away as you can hold it. Study it for a minute.

Now, prop it up; and walk back 6 feet. Look at it again.

Does it look different now—from that distance? Are there features that perhaps you did not see at closer range?

What you are doing now *physically*—i.e., looking at the page from a detached viewpoint—the skillful reader does *psychologically* every time he glances at a page of print. He looks down on it, as it were, from a considerable distance. By so doing he conditions himself to look first at the *whole* page, its *gestalt*, its telltale characteristics, its typographical terrain, its clues for effective and rapid reading. Contrary to the popular belief, the expert reader does not at once plunge into the wilderness of print. He does not begin to read the first five seconds he sees a page. He merely looks—meaningfully, inquiringly. He seeks to get the "out-there" view.

It's HOW You Look That Makes the Difference!

From what has been said thus far, it may be apparent that what a reader does in the first five seconds that he glances at a page determines whether or not he knows what to do with that page. Tell most people to read a page, a chapter, or a book, and what happens? They start at the first word and read, word by word, straight through to the last word. By so doing they lose perspective; they see nothing; they comprehend little. They have no idea of the structure or the architecture of the thought or of the overall contour of the author's idea pattern. All they see are words, words, words. And this, they think, is reading. It is, in fact, little more than visual grubbing.

After the first sentence or two the average reader has lost his way. He plods aimlessly, reading words and yet more words, remembering fragments of fact, and comprehending poorly or not at all—comprehending, that is, in the literal sense of the term, which means "to catch hold of or seize broadly."

Look at This Page at Close Range

Think now of this page as receding from you—to arm's length, or further. Don't *actually* move it any further than proper reading distance, but look at it as though it were some distance away. Try to see the whole page. What happens? You are aware of your eyes alighting on one feature, then on another. But try to see it all in a glance. What do you see, or what should you see? If an expert reader were to advise you, what features would he counsel you to look for on a page of print? Let's list the items:

1. *Look at the heading.* There, streaming banner-like across the top of the page is the headline of this chapter: "What to Do with a Page of Print." Of all those words in the heading, the word "What" is perhaps the most important. It means "the exact thing." What precisely will you do with a page of print? That question, you see, gives focus for all the rest of your reading. From now on, you will be looking for "the exact thing" to do with the page.

2. *Look at the subheadings.* The subheadings at once suggest that the larger division of the writing is broken down into lesser units of thought organization. Of course, at this point, the really alert reader might flip through the rest of the chapter, reading only the subheadings as they come up one after another throughout the chapter. Try it with this chapter. You will suddenly be aware of a running chain of thought.

3. *Look for the paragraph indentations.* Even the most casual observer must notice this feature of the page. The printer, the editor, the author have all conspired to make the page easy reading for you. To see the paragraph notches down the left-hand margin of the text is to begin to see the more closely connected thought structure of the page. Here is the master key to comprehension. In actual practice, however, readers are seldom conscious of paragraph indentations. Yet, every time you drop into one of these notches and begin reading another paragraph you make an assault on a new thought or attack another aspect of an old one.

Note how the four brief paragraphs with which this chapter began gave you, first, a blanket command (Look at this page); next, a specific suggestion (Hold it away from you . . .); then, the proposal that you back away from it (Now, prop it up; and walk back 6 feet); and, finally, the fourth brief paragraph invited you to reflect upon the result of the prior actions (Does it look different now . . .). Actually, there were four ideas here in the sense of four separate adjustments of the reader to the page. Then followed a discussion on the meaning of what you were just asked to do (What you are doing now physically . . .).

Paragraphing was devised so that the author might let the reader know where a thought begins or where the development of a new phase of it commences.

4. *Look at the sizes of the various blocks of prose.* Note how

the paragraph sizes vary. Some of them are only one line in length. These are high-powered units that release much energy in a brief burst of print. Others are longer and more involved. These release thought energy much more slowly. Here the author takes time to unfold the intricacies and sophistication of the thought so that it may be clearly comprehensible to the reader. Take the fifth paragraph at the beginning of this chapter, for instance. Here the author is trying to show you the *raison d'être* for what he has categorically asked you to do in the first four paragraphs. The fifth paragraph is a kind of "come, now, let us reason together" to see what we have been doing and why. The paragraph is longer than those preceding it: it takes longer to reason matters out than it does to command acts to be done.

5. *Look for type-face differences.* When an author wishes to say something with special emphasis, or when he considers that the reader should note particularly some word or group of words, he usually puts these in italics or in a different type face than that which is used in the text. With a little skill and attention any reader can see and note at once these italicized islands within the text. Sometimes an author uses quotation marks in a similar way—to mark the unusual, the out-of-the-ordinary, the bizarre in expression.

Glance at the Page to Set the Stage

A glance at the page, therefore, will tell you much. Noting the obvious will set the stage for further reading action. A few seconds of time efficiently invested can clear the runway for a take-off into the full meaning of the text.

Let's look back now and do exactly what we have been suggesting. Let's look at the self-evident features on the pages which you have just read. This is what you should have done before you plunged into the text. Down the page your eyes should have swept, touching the text lightly; and in the first ten seconds of your reading time, you should have seen the following headings and subheads:

WHAT TO DO WITH A PAGE OF PRINT

Look! It's *how* you look that makes the difference. Look at this page at close range. First, look at the heading. Second, look at the subheadings. Third, look for the paragraph indentations. Fourth, look at the sizes of the various blocks of prose. Fifth, look for type-face differences. Glance at the page to set the stage.

Here, you see, is the outline. If you see no more than this you will have a head start. In one-sixth of a minute you will have the author's thought packed in a nutshell. Actually, in ten seconds, to this point in the chapter you have traversed exactly 1,360 words. Not that you have read anything in connected sentences and continuous prose. You have merely skimmed. But at this rate, assuming that the above outline is all that you want, you have covered these pages at the astounding rate of nearly 8,200 words a minute!

This is an escape velocity that is quite adequate to remove you from the dragging effects of the heavy print on the page. Like an astronaut, once you have established verbal weightlessness you are now at ease to inspect the details of the page from a more expansive and comprehensive viewpoint.

A Word, Now, about Rate of Reading

Perhaps here is the place to think realistically about the matter of rate of reading. The conventional way of measuring reading rate is in terms of words per minute. And this is acceptable so long as we understand what we mean by this term. If such an expression presumes that every word is of equal importance in the reading process, the presumption is wrong. If it assumes that you must read every word with equal attention in order to "get the thought," this, of course, is not the case. If it further presumes that there is only one product in reading—the full meaning and *all* the overtones of every word upon the page—this is likewise unrealistic in the light of many of today's reading needs. Such detailed reading may be desirable for the reading of poetry and contracts, but it is not generally necessary for many of our daily reading chores, including magazines and newspapers.

Let us not think, therefore, primarily of so many words per minute, although this is perhaps the most convenient and conventional way of measuring your rate of reading; but let us conceive of reading rate as the speed of absorption of ideas. That, of course, is something quite different; and is very difficult to measure. One word, for instance, may contain a whole idea, or it may take a dozen words to convey an equal burden of thought.

The printed word contains many variables, and some of these are related to the personal equation and are difficult to capture or evaluate. Among such are the style of the author, the purpose of the reader, the importance of what is being read, the sophistication of the subject matter, the skillfulness of the reader in dealing with the page of print. All these variables are as much a part of the reading of the page as the print itself, and any one or a combination of factors may influence the rate at which the reading of the page will be dispatched.

We see, therefore, that to place inordinate emphasis on rate of reading is comparable to placing undue stress on speed in driving a car. To do so is perhaps to encourage recklessness and to magnify out of all proportion one element in a constellation of many factors: speed, safety, road conditions, and other considerations. It is to think of only one aspect of reading as though it were all important and an end in itself.

Manifestly, this is not the case. Like a skillful driver, you should aim to get through the maze of print as quickly and

yet as effectively as possible in keeping with all the other
considerations which may influence your speed. But, as there
are methods of making haste safely on the highway, so there
are comparable methods of getting to one's destination along
the avenues of print with least effort and minimal loss of time.
It is to that goal that the rest of this book is dedicated.

Develop Mastery in Reading the Paragraph

Your master key to both speed and comprehension is to
develop consummate skill in learning to read the paragraph
effectively. Before, however, you can learn to *read* the paragraph, you must learn to *see* the paragraph. One glance at
the page, and the paragraphs upon it should stand out in bold
relief. In a flash you should spot the paragraphs and appraise
their thought power in terms of their length and structure.
All meaningful prose conveys its thought content by means of
the paragraph as a basic unit of writing. It is, therefore, of
greatest importance that you learn to master the paragraph
form at the very outset.

What Is a Paragraph?

A paragraph is a way of thinking.

It is a way of stating a thought so that the reader might see
exactly what that thought means. Conventional paragraphs
usually consist of two parts:

1. *The principal idea,* which is usually contained in a sentence called the "main-idea" or "topic" sentence; and
2. *The subsidiary details* which enlarge upon or illustrate
   the basic idea by means of a series of sentences that repeat,
   explain, contrast, or justify the thought contained in the
   main-idea sentence.

Paragraphs are, therefore, windows through which the
reader peers into the inner meaning of the author's thought
and sees what significance it contains.

Paragraphs Reflect the Way We Think

Human beings think according to certain basic rules and patterns. Paragraphs are written the way they are because we think the way we do. They are usually oriented so that the thought flows in one of two directions: either away from or toward the generalized and main idea. To see more clearly the flow of thought and the fundamental patterns of thinking, let us take several hypothetical examples. First, we shall illustrate the thought flow away from the main idea. Consider this chain of events:

I go out for a meeting at the Dorchester Club at 8 in the evening. My wife expects me home by 11:30. At 3 the next morning, I stealthily insert the key in the lock, open the door, and steal into the hall.

A voice descends the stairway.

"Paul, is that you?"

"Yes," I reply, "I couldn't get here any sooner!"

(Note, my first utterance is a generalization. Now I supply the details to support that first general statement and main idea.)

"You see," I explain, "I left the club at ten forty-five and drove to Walker's Corners, where the car stalled. After unsuccessfully grinding at the starter, I walked about half a mile to a roadside telephone booth to call a garage and to let you know what had happened; but the phone had a sign on it, 'Out of order.' I then tried tinkering with the car to find the trouble. By this time, it was almost midnight, and so I raised the hood on the car and walked back to the club to telephone. No one was around and the club was dark. I have been walking the eleven miles from Dorchester to here since twelve-thirty."

Structurally, the thought pattern of that paragraph looks something like this:

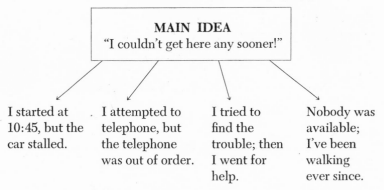

MAIN IDEA
"I couldn't get here any sooner!"

| I started at 10:45, but the car stalled. | I attempted to telephone, but the telephone was out of order. | I tried to find the trouble; then I went for help. | Nobody was available; I've been walking ever since. |

Note how every detail darts from the main idea, pointing to reason after reason that supports the main thought. Standing alone, the main idea would have had little specific meaning. In fact, there may have been a thousand conceivable reasons why I could not have arrived home before 3 in the morning. My wife was perhaps even thinking of some of them! By means of certain specific facts, however, I established the principal statement within a limiting framework which expressly confined the possible reasons and, as a result, clarified my principal statement as to why I could not get home any earlier than I did.

The Deductive Pattern

Now, that was not only a satisfactory explanation; it was a well-structured paragraph also. It, furthermore, represents the way most of us think most of the time. Our thought process begins with a generalization; then, we proceed outward from that generalized statement to specific details and explicit facts.

Note how many times every day you encounter this same type of thinking. The boss wants you to assume a new responsibility. He calls you into his office, therefore, and says: "Jim, I have always felt that you were one of the most reliable men in our firm." That's a big statement, and it may take you momentarily off guard. But it's more than that; it's a generalization which he uses as a springboard from which he takes off to tell you what makes you so valuable and why he wants you to assume the added responsibility. His argument might be represented graphically as follows:

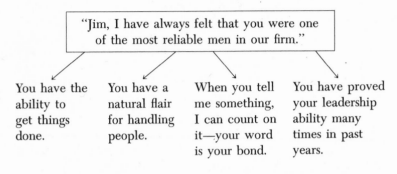

"Jim, I have always felt that you were one of the most reliable men in our firm."

| You have the ability to get things done. | You have a natural flair for handling people. | When you tell me something, I can count on it—your word is your bond. | You have proved your leadership ability many times in past years. |

What is important is the *direction* of the thought flow: from the generalization outward—away from the main idea toward the specific details. Such thinking is called *deductive* thinking (*de* = from + *duct* = leading). It literally describes what happens in the process of thinking—a leading outward *from* the central idea to the supporting incidents and clenching details.

Inspect any page, and you will find that most of the paragraphs are deductively developed: the topic sentence—the most important thought—then, the details. Because most of the time we *think* that way, consequently, we *write* that way.

The Inductive Pattern

Let us now consider another type of thought-motion within the paragraph. We shall reverse the process:

As a lad I recall coming home from school one day and encountering my father, who greeted me with these words:

"Son, I understand that you have not been doing too well in school lately. Your report card arrived today, and I note: arithmetic, D; spelling, F; history, F; and conduct, 'unsatisfactory.' Your mother tells me she has repeatedly asked you to mow the lawn, and you have failed to do it. You were to carry in the wood from the woodpile [we lived on a farm] and you have not done that either. And I hear that last night you dipped the cat's paws in the glue! And so, let us go now, you and I, out to the woodshed, where I will teach you a lesson you'll not soon forget!"

Note how the punch line—the main idea—comes last. This, too, is a good paragraph, but its pattern is an inversion of the examples we have just given: a boy's shortcomings are recalled, item by item, and then all of the details nose-dive into the concluding statement of the main thought.

Structured like the examples above, the thought pattern of this paragraph might look something like this:

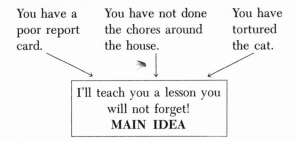

You have a poor report card.

You have not done the chores around the house.

You have tortured the cat.

> I'll teach you a lesson you will not forget!
> **MAIN IDEA**

Instead of flowing outward from the principal statement, as in the deductive pattern, in this paragraph the main idea originates from a confluence of specific instances. Here the thought flow is *in* toward the main idea. Such a pattern we call the *inductive* (*in* = in, into, toward + *duct* = leading) method of paragraph development.

The Case of the Missing Main Idea

Occasionally, however, you will find the main idea neither in the first place nor in the last place in the paragraph. It may even be omitted entirely. In such instances the sensitivity of the reader should alert him to the drift of the thought. In such paragraphs, the reader keeps saying to himself: These are all merely details, but through them all the author is attempting to say one thing. What is that one thought which the author is trying to express? Finally, as the details multiply, the reader will begin to discern the overall main idea that the author is attempting to express. For example, take this paragraph:

> Some people read ineffectively because they need glasses. Others do not read well because they are thinking of something else, and they are not paying attention to what their eyes are seeing on the page. With such readers the words never reach any conscious awareness in the brain. Still other people read poorly because of bad reading habits or because they have never been taught the proper methods of extracting thought effortlessly from the printed page. Finally, there are those who read poorly because they have such limited vocabularies that their lack of word power makes it impossible for them to gain full comprehension of the meaning.

What now is the thought toward which all these statements are drifting? It is the main-idea statement *Poor reading has many possible causes.*

Find the Main Idea, Then—Keep Track of It!

To locate only the main idea is not enough, important as that may be. There is much more to effective reading. To read well means to know exactly *what* is happening within a given paragraph *at any given moment.* It is to find the main idea and then to keep track of it as it winds and twists and turns throughout the whole paragraph.

The successful reader keeps constantly oriented to the milieu of print. He keeps in close contact with the thought complex that lies beneath the words. He is fully aware of what is transpiring within the realm of the printed page.

To read well means to be aware. It means being continually alert to the structure of the thought within each of the sentences upon the page. It means not losing contact with the nuances of meaning.

This carries us at once into the very heart of the paragraph. Observe, sentence by sentence, what happens when an author, once having stated a main idea, proceeds to develop it in order to show the reader what he means. For, having stated an idea, an author can then do only four things with it. He can:

1. Repeat it: rephrase the idea in other words.

   (By the way, how acute is your paragraph sense? Were you aware that the second paragraph in this subsection was of this type? It was!)

2. Contrast it: show the meaning of the idea by comparing it with its opposite.

   (Again, how sensitive were you? Did you notice a paragraph thus far that employed techniques 1 and 2? Look at the third paragraph in this subsection.)

3. Exemplify it: give an example to illustrate the idea.

4. Justify it: give a reason to support or vindicate a statement.

And these are the only four types of sentences that a paragraph can contain which relate to the main idea. This is all that an author can possibly do with an idea.

Occasionally, however, the author may make a statement which falls within the general area of the thought but which is not logically a part of it. Such statements are paragraph "filler." They have no organic unity with the main stream of the thought of the paragraph. These "wild shoots," these tangential sentences—which we might call "dud" sentences— should be clearly recognized as such. Like the proverbial sore thumb, they protrude from the logic of the main-idea sentences of the paragraph. The alert reader will recognize them instantly. Some minds, however, seem constitutionally incapable of being logical.

Are you alert? Did you notice that last sentence of the preceding paragraph was a "dud"? It had nothing at all to do with the main thought of the paragraph.

Consider the following paragraph. As you read it see whether you can identify exactly the function of each sentence in terms of the functional categories outlined above:

> To read well means to be aware. Awareness is a personal asset: either you have it, or you don't have it. Good reading demands that the reader be keenly alert to every feature of the page, to every nuance of the thought. The successful reader does not woolgather while he reads. Instead, he is constantly aware of the main thought and what the author is doing with it. Is he illustrating it? Repeating it? Contrasting it? Justifying it? Because the efficient reader saves time as well as getting more for the time which he does invest, it pays him to be alert to every movement of the thought, to every feature of the page. Alertness and good reading go hand in hand.

HERE IS THAT SAME PARAGRAPH ANALYZED:

[1] To read well means to be aware.	1. The main idea.
[2] Awareness is a personal asset: either you have it, or you don't have it.	2. A "dud" sentence that has nothing to do with the main thought of the paragraph.
[3] Good reading demands that the reader be keenly alert to every feature of the page, to every nuance of the thought.	3. A repetition of the main idea. Read this sentence, then read sentence no. 1.

⁴ The successful reader does not wool-gather while he reads. | ⁵ Instead, he is constantly aware of the main thought and what the author is doing with it.

⁶ Is he illustrating it? ⁷ Repeating it? ⁸ Contrasting it? ⁹ Justifying it?

¹⁰ Because the efficient reader saves time as well as getting more for the time which he does invest, it pays him to be alert to every movement of the thought, to every feature of the page.

¹¹ Alertness and good reading go hand in hand.

4. A contrasting sentence. It tells what the successful reader does *not* do.

5. Repetition of the main idea. "Instead" reverses the contrasting negative of the preceding sentence.

6,7,8,9. All examples of what being aware means. Here we see an example of how the mind of the aware reader asks questions, how he probes the text.

10. Justifying the main idea. Here the author gives a reason why one should read well and be alert.

11. Repetition of the main idea (a concluding and summarizing statement).

Wake Up—and Think!

To read well, therefore, your mind must attack the page with a constant barrage of questions and observations.

Let's see a transcript of what might happen in the mind of an efficient reader, as he glances at a page.

> "Subhead, eh? Wonder what the other subheads are. [He thumbs back to see where this subhead stands with respect to those that have gone before and those that follow it.]
> "Paragraphs? Four. Short, not too fully developed.

"Main idea? Let's see—first sentence? Right! First sentence. [He notes each of the following first sentences. They make sense logically and sequentially.]

"O.K. Now to look carefully at the paragraph structure. First sentence? Oh, yes. Main idea. Second sentence? Sure, an example. Illustrates the main thought. Third sentence? Another example. Next sentence—contrasting idea: he's been telling me what it is, now he's telling me what it is *not*. That helps; I can see by contrast what he means. Last sentence? Repetition: a restatement of the main thought. Thoughtwise, we're back to where we started."

To read this, of course, is like seeing slow-motion photography. Actually, everything in the above transcript happens at the lightning speed of thought. It happens so fast, in fact, that you describe it by saying that you see the paragraph in a glance. This is not so, but most readers never stop to analyze what does go on when they face a page of print—especially, if they know what to do with it.

To read with a mind that is alive, alert, and working is to read intelligently. It is to comprehend meaningfully, to know exactly what is happening in each line of the printed page.

Think of a Paragraph as a Whirlpool

A paragraph is a dynamic unit of writing. It contains within its structure motion and countermotion, the ebb and flow of thought. To read a paragraph well demands alertness and mental activity. You must have all your wits about you, and you must look sharp to keep on the *qui vive* as you attempt to follow that thought and what is happening to it.

Study a whirlpool. It is a complex of motion: currents, countercurrents, stationary vortices which turn slowly, demonstrating motion without progress; and then the sudden onward, outward rush of waters vying with the onsweep of the main stream.

Now, a paragraph is like a whirlpool. For the way to look at a whirlpool is to see all its motions against the onward, resistless flow of the main current. Likewise, the way to grasp the full meaning of the paragraph is to comprehend the complex motions of the several subordinate thoughts as these flow contrary to or along with the onward surge of the main idea.

The main idea is the main stream of the thought. Every other sentence—each subordinate current within the paragraph—is significant only in relation to the forward, onward flow of the basic thought.

To know not only what the words mean, but what is happening to the thought at any given moment in any particular place within the paragraph, this is the beginning of comprehension. When, for example, an author contrasts an idea he is, in effect, setting up a countercurrent to the main flow of the thought stream. If, on the other hand, he repeats the idea, he gives it additional impetus, sending the thought rushing headlong in the direction of the main flow of the principal thought.

To keep the figure of the stream just a little longer, think of the repetition of the idea as the tumbling of water over a rapids. When water does this, it seems to gain force and power because it is impelled onward with redoubled speed. When a thought is repeated, it likewise redoubles the force of the main idea of the paragraph.

Whether in stream or paragraph, there are sometimes pools where there is little onward motion. Like quiet eddies within a stream, the thought within a paragraph occasionally seems merely to revolve, having no forward progress; but it turns round and round so that you may see the author's idea and consider it more leisurely as he illuminates it by an example or undergirds it with a reason.

Earlier in this chapter we discussed the four ways by which an author can amplify a main idea. As a built-in feature, a well-written paragraph usually employs certain words or phrases which cue the sensitive reader exactly as to what the author is doing with the thought. Furthermore, such expressions are so unobtrusive that the average reader seldom notices them. And, too, he flashes across these words with such ease that, unless he looks for them specifically, they will not intrude themselves upon his awareness. Since, then, these words are so important, every reader should recognize them on sight; and, moreover, he should note their specific effect upon the meaning of the particular sentence that he is reading. In short, these directional—or perhaps a better term might be "orientational"—words are so very important in keeping the reader cued to the motion and consequently the meaning of the thought in the paragraph that every efficient reader should be alert to them and to their functional purpose in increasing reading ease and aiding comprehension.

And what are these words? Have you been aware that in the last paragraph, which contained six sentences, *five* of these orientational words were employed?

Look again at the preceding paragraph as it has been condensed and is reprinted below. Note the effect of the words in the boldface type in keeping you oriented to the constantly forward movement of the main thought.

The Condensed Paragraph	Comment
[1] Earlier we discussed four ways by which an author amplifies a main idea. [2] As a built-in feature, *a well-written paragraph employs words or phrases which cue the reader as to what the author is doing.* [3] **Furthermore,** such expressions are so unobtrusive that the average reader seldom notices them.	1. A dud sentence, merely recalling previous discussion in the book. 2. The main idea: the rest of the paragraph will talk about these words or phrases which cue the reader. 3. *Furthermore:* the first of the cue words, meaning *and now, more of the same, in addition.*

⁴ **And, too,** he flashes across these words with such ease that they do not intrude upon his awareness. ⁵ **Since** these words are so important, every reader should recognize them; **moreover,** he should note their effect on the thought. ⁶ **In short,** these cue words are so important that every reader should be alert to them.

4. *And, too:* another cue expression, urging the thought on and still further onward.

5. *Since:* a cue word that indicates a reason. Since means *because:* "because these words are so important. . . ." *Moreover:* meaning *in addition now to what has already been said.* This word nudges the thought still further.

6. *In short:* The final cue word that says to the reader, in effect, "We shall now present in capsulated form the gist of what we have been discussing thus far."

Some of the cue words in the paragraph that we have just analyzed were forward-oriented: *furthermore, and too, moreover;* other cue words asked you to pause while a reason was advanced or a summing up was made. If we refer again to the four basic ways in which an author can manipulate his idea, we find that it is possible also to categorize the orientational words under four headings: (1) those cue words which repeat the idea, suggest progress, or show that the thought is moving forward following the momentum of the main thought; (2) those which reverse the thought or contrast it with the main idea; (3) those that orient the reader so that he expects an example or an illustration of what the main idea means; or (4) those words and phrases which tell the reader that the author is about to justify what he has already said by offering a reason or presenting supportive evidence.

In the following list are some of the most common cue words and phrases in each category. Each of these affects the flow of thought within the paragraph in a specific way. Illustrative sentences show the effect of the orientational word.

Words That Suggest to the Reader the Idea of Furtherance, Repetition, or Addition

Word	Meaning	Illustrative Use
AGAIN	once more, besides	*Again,* let us look at the matter this way.
ALSO	likewise, too, in addition	*Also,* we might add, it is not important.
AND	also, in addition, plus, furthermore	*And,* it looks suspiciously like extortion.
AS WELL AS	equivalent to, no less than, in addition to	He gave of his wealth *as well as* his talent.
BESIDES	in addition (to), moreover	*Besides,* what more is there to say? [Implies a previous discussion.]
FURTHER, FURTHERMORE	to a greater extent, moreover, in addition	I think him an excellent workman, *furthermore,* I think he should be promoted.
IN ADDITION TO	further than, beyond, more than	*In addition to* what we have already done, we should honor this man for his loyalty.
MOREOVER	in addition to what has already been said	Good reading depends upon efficient skills; *moreover,* it depends upon the application of those skills each time you read.

Words That Emphasize the Countercurrents of the Thought

Word	Meaning	Illustrative Use
ALTHOUGH	albeit, in spite of the fact that	*Although* he is rich, he is not happy.
AS A MATTER OF FACT	The phrase implies that what has been said is *not* a matter of fact.	There are, *as a matter of fact,* places on the surface of the earth where it is colder than at the North Pole.
BUT	on the contrary, yet	I am old, *but* he is young.
EITHER . . . OR	Denotes a choice of alternatives	*Either* we will leave tomorrow *or* we will not go at all.
EVEN, EVEN IF (THOUGH)	moreover, though it may seem improbable	The playing of the game is worthwhile, *even if* you never win.
HOWEVER	nevertheless, yet, but	I shall not reject his offer; *however,* I am not sure I shall accept it.
IN SPITE OF	despite, notwithstanding, regardless of	I will go, *in spite of* storm, delay, and all conspiracy of Nature.
INSTEAD OF	in place of, rather than	He telephoned him, *instead of* writing to him.
NEVERTHELESS	notwithstanding, in spite of that, however	We are at peace with all men; *nevertheless,* war could break out at any moment.

NOTWITHSTAND-ING	in spite of, nevertheless, although	He simply will not believe it, *notwithstanding* all the evidence to the contrary.
ON THE OTHER HAND	to the contrary, from a different standpoint	He felt that he should tell the boss; *on the other hand,* he had given his word that he would not breathe it to anyone.
RATHER (THAN)	on the contrary, an alternate choice	I would *rather* have peace of mind *than* fame and fortune.
REGARDLESS	without heed for, unmindful of (suggests a deliberate position in the face of contrary facts)	I will not change my mind, *regardless* of how long you argue or how conclusively you demonstrate the facts.
TO THE CONTRARY, CONTRARY TO	to the opposite (effect or result), on the other side	Greece was one of the few true democracies of history; *contrary to* popular opinion, the United States is not a democracy but a republic.
UNLESS	if not, in any case other than, except that	We will go tomorrow *unless* it rains; in which case, the trip will be cancelled.
WHEREAS	while on the contrary	He spoke freely, *whereas* she was evasive.
YET	nevertheless, however	The air is cold, *yet* the sun is warm.

Expressions That Prepare the Reader for an Illustration or an Example

Word	Meaning	Illustrative Use
AS	like, in the same manner that	Repeating an idea is *as* the tumbling of water over a rapids.
FOR EXAMPLE	as an illustration of, as a specific instance illustrating	Think, *for example*, of reading as of driving over varied terrain with varying traffic conditions.
FOR INSTANCE	as an illustration or example	Take the matter of speed of reading: one should read, *for instance*, with the same flexibility of speed as one drives his car according to varying road conditions.
IF	on condition that, supposing, contrary to actual fact	*If* he knows when he is well off, he will push the situation no farther.
LIKE	similar to, comparable to	Life, it has been said, is *like* a stream.
SPECIFICALLY, TO BE SPECIFIC	definitely, explicitly, peculiar to or characteristic of something	Certain rocks have become known the world over; *to be specific*, consider Plymouth Rock or the Rock of Gibraltar.

Expressions That Prepare the Reader for
A Reason or for Supportive Evidence

Word	*Meaning*	*Illustrative Use*
BECAUSE	for the reason that	The corn is stunted and the grain is prematurely ripe, *because* we have had no rain for months.
FOR	because, because of	Possession begets possession, *for* no sooner do we have one thing than we want another.
FORASMUCH AS	since, because, inasmuch as, seeing that	*Forasmuch as* my candle burns at both ends, it will not last the night.
SINCE	because, forasmuch as	Let us not waste time on useless books; *since* there is so much to read, so little time for reading.
THEREFORE	thus, consequently	I do not know, *therefore,* I cannot say.

One further word should be said about these orientational words and phrases. In actual practice, an author may omit the cue word if, without it, the function of the sentence is obvious to the skillful reader. Such a situation frequently happens. When it does, you must sense the relationship that the author assumed any adept reader would sense and which the author intended but did not express.

Not Everything Is a Paragraph That Looks Like One

Appearances are deceptive. Authors are whimsical. And, not everything *is* a paragraph that looks like one.

The reader, therefore, must always be in command. In facing a page of print, for example, nothing replaces the agile, active, inquiring, analyzing mind of a reader who knows exactly what the author is saying because that reader knows exactly what the author is doing with the thought and, hence, precisely what is transpiring on the page.

(Incidentally, have you been in command? Or, has the somewhat complex structure of the thought in the last two paragraphs eluded you? At the close of this section you will have an opportunity to test your "command status." Keep alert, therefore, from here on. Watch for reading booby traps.)

Indentations in the left margin of print usually signal the beginning of a new thought. But, this is not always true. Quite to the contrary, such paragraph indentations may mean, for example, that the author is merely providing "reader relief."

Great blocks of print are depressing to many readers. They see them as ponderous and forbidding. Authors know this. They, therefore, sometimes break up a longer discussion into subdiscussions or perhaps an extended paragraph into subparagraphs.

Reasons may be detached from the facts which they logically justify. Examples, moreover, may be separated by paragraph division from the principles which they illustrate. Logically, however, all material should be in the same prose package with the other material with which it is inseparably linked. But, this may form inordinately long paragraph structures which, because of their very length, may have psychologically adverse effects on the reader.

It is psychologically advantageous, therefore, occasionally to separate integrally connected parts of a discussion, although to do so places a greater burden upon the skill and ability of the reader, his acuteness and sense of awareness of what is happening on the page.

(*Now turn to page 168. There you will have the opportunity to test your reading skill and ability, your own sense of acuteness and awareness of what has been happening in the above section.*)

Reading for Maximum Awareness of the Thought

From what we have said thus far, you may have inferred that perhaps paragraphs should be read merely superficially. That is not so. Most paragraphs are to be read intelligently and with full awareness of their thought. Yet, most people just read. Some readers are even insensitive to the left-hand notches in the column of print that signal the beginning of a new paragraph. Those who are aware of paragraph beginnings sometimes also just read—losing all perspective, so that the sentences sooner or later level out for them into a dull monotony of print. This frequently results in merely reading words without a vivid awareness as to the way in which those words are organized into illuminating, thought-bearing units.

To read a paragraph for its fullest meaning is to read with a mind led by an interrogation point!

But how does one do this? Where can you find an interrogation point that can lead the mind?

Try this. Read the first sentence of the paragraph—assuming, of course, that the first sentence is the topic sentence. Then, enter the question mark! Immediately after you have read the topic sentence, ask yourself: "What does that mean?" Then read to find out. Preface the reading of each of the other sentences in the paragraph with the phrase, "It means . . . ." Then, read to find out what it *does* mean. You will find that the topic sentence gives you the main idea and that, in a well-constructed paragraph, every other sentence supplements this main idea by telling you in part specifically what that main idea means.

Part of your success as a reader will depend upon the unique ways in which you visualize the thought within the paragraph. Thought is structural; and if you see it correctly, you must see it in structural relationship.

Take, for example, the condensed version of the paragraph which you will find on page 48, and which was discussed there. Now, think of the main idea as the topmost idea in the thought structure. The corollary ideas of the paragraph are related to the main idea through the verbal formula suggested above. Regarded in such manner, on page 50 is the way that paragraph would appear.

But some minds function naturally in another way. We do not all think alike. Some readers naturally think in terms of an outline. You may wish to think of the data arrangement in this way. If so, the paragraph cited would appear as follows:

I. A well-written paragraph employs words or phrases which cue the reader. [*What does that mean? It means that . . .*]
   A. Such expressions are unobtrusive.
   B. The reader flashes across these words or phrases easily.
   C. Every reader should recognize these words and note their effect on the thought.
   D. Readers should be alert.

With these several tools, the paragraph should no longer appear to you as an enigma. It should readily yield to you its meaning. It should unfold the ideas which the author has placed there, and which it will be your pleasure to discover.

But there is still more in learning what to do with a page of print. We shall discuss this in the next section.

MAIN IDEA
A well-written paragraph
employs words or phrases
which cue the reader.

What
does
that
mean?

It means that . . .

1.
Such expressions
are so unobtrusive
that the average
reader seldom
notices them.

4.
Cue words are so
important that
every reader
should be alert to
them.

2.
He flashes across
these words with
such ease that they
do not intrude
upon his awareness.

3.
(Because) these
words are so impor-
tant, every reader
should recognize
them (and) note
their effect on
the thought.

Dots and Dashes That Help You Read Better

Try your reading skill on this:

THAT THAT IS IS THAT IS IS THAT THAT IS
BUT THAT THAT IS NOT IS NOT THAT THAT IS.

Having trouble? You shouldn't have! For when you read that sentence aright it makes perfect sense.

But it *is* confusing, isn't it?

And at this point, one fact should be abundantly clear: Words upon the page are, by themselves, not enough to convey the meaning. Fast, efficient, precise reading demands still another feature upon the page to aid your comprehension. Furthermore, this feature is an integral part of every page that you read. We call it punctuation—the little dots and dashes that turn mere words into meaningful sentences.

By the way, have you figured out that sentence yet? Keep working at it, but if it gives you too much trouble, why not turn to page 190 in the Answer Key, and there you will find it completely and meaningfully punctuated.

Without these little dots and dashes on the page, the printed word would lose much of its meaning and reading would become an extremely difficult task.

The history of punctuation is interesting. Originally, in the ancient papyri manuscripts the letters ran on continuously, without a break or interruption, one close against another. Let us reproduce in English what you very well might have seen in a Greek manuscript. Try your comprehension on this:

DIDYOUEVERSEEABUNDANCEONTHETABLE

And, now, what do you suppose that says? How would you like to readthisbookifthelettersallrantogetherlikethis? Yet, the ancient "books" (manuscripts) were written in exactly that manner.

By the way, have you figured out what that sentence says? If it bothers you too much, turn to page 190 and read the comment in the Answer Key.

Actually, punctuation originated with the ancient Greek grammarians, perhaps in Roman times. One of the first marks to be used was the interrogation point—and, incidentally, "pointing" was the old name for punctuating. It means originally a dot in writing, and to this day we still retain this meaning in the expression "decimal *point.*"

If you think about punctuation, you will readily realize that it is composed of combinations of three elements only: a dot (.), a modified dot with a "tail" (,), and a short line (—).

From these three "points," all the rest have been derived. Place a period over a comma, and you have a semicolon. Our semicolon was, in fact, the interrogation point of the old Greek grammarians; and only through extensive evolution has it become what it now is—an "s" in reverse with a dot under it (?). Two dots, one above the other (:), provide the colon; while a vertical dash with a dot below it (!) tells the reader that what has been said is an exclamation or has been said by way of surprise. Finally, a pair of commas upside down before a group of words, paired with a similar set in conventional position and located slightly above the line (" "), informs the reader that what is between them are the exact words of another.

Because these marks tell so much about the nature of the thought, express moods, or indicate what the author is desirous of the reader knowing *in addition to the words,* every reader ought to be alert and adept at translating the meaning of these various marks that appear in the line of print. They are the dots and dashes that help you to read the page with greater speed and increased comprehension.

Yet, it is amazing how few readers know, clearly and unerringly, exactly how these marks of punctuation affect the thought, and are knowledgeable as to the effect of this "pointing" upon the thought content.

Ask most people, for instance, what they expect when suddenly they see a colon in a line of print. You may be interested in the variety of answers that you will get. Likewise, to most readers the dash is a similar enigma.

When an engineer brings a train into Grand Central Station in New York, down in the tunnel under Park Avenue, he threads his way among a labyrinth of tracks and amid a bewildering array of multicolored signal lights: green, amber, red, blue, purple—all winking at him from overhead or beside the track. Each light is meaningful and is telling the engineer how to proceed so that he may bring his train to the station platform in safety and with greatest dispatch.

Just so are the marks of punctuation. Along the lines of print these signals stand, telling the reader how to proceed. The presence of one of them is an indication of what to expect of the thought within that particular sentence. As the skillful reader proceeds along the line of print, his eyes note these punctuational signals, which flash their messages to his brain so that he may move quickly and effortlessly down the page with greatest degree of comprehension and maximum awareness as to the meaning of its content.

Most readers are largely unaware of the important role that punctuation serves or how much of it is found on a normal page. Take any page—this page, for example—and with a pencil circle all of the punctuation marks: the periods, commas, semicolons, quotation marks, apostrophes, colons, hyphens, dashes, and parentheses. You will be amazed at the abundance of these "points" on a single page. They are the marks that guide you swiftly and expeditiously to the fullness of the author's thought.

How, then, is punctuation employed on the page? Each mark has its own purpose to fulfill, its own function to perform. Here are some of the more common uses.

Signals That Bring You to a Full Stop

The period. The most common mark of punctuation, and perhaps the best understood, is the period. Wherever you find it, it means always the same thing. It is a signal calling for a full stop—a terminal point in the thought chain.

So important, in fact, is this point that it is triply indicated: the period shows where one thought is terminated; then the printer leaves a double space—the width of an em quad—to separate the sentences; and, finally, the towering capital letter, standing athwart the line of type, announces to the reader that here begins a new thought unit.

When you began this chapter you were advised to hold the page at arm's length and to look at the page with a detached view. Try that technique again. Look down on the page. Try to see only the periods, the blank spaces, and the accompanying capital letters. Better yet, take a page which you have not yet attempted to read and circle every period. It will emphasize their presence. It will also indicate the various places on the page where one thought ends and another one begins, and it will show you the relative length of each thought unit.

Furthermore, the application of this information is vital to rapid, intelligent reading. As a general rule, the longer the sentence the more involved the thought which it purports to convey and, consequently, the more complex and difficult it is to comprehend. Therefore, long sentences are generally more difficult to read than are shorter ones. Rudolf Flesch, Robert Gunning, and others have used this fact as a basic assumption in developing their formulas of readability. The principle involved is a psychological one: the more wordage the mind must carry before it comes to a point where the thought is resolved, the more skill is required to cope with this "verbal burden." Conversely, a succession of very short sentences are not the easiest to read, either. They cause problems. Many readers dislike them. They hinder. They clutter the page. They inhibit the full stride. They fragment the prose. Thought becomes disconnected. Reading tends to be jerky. Thought comes in tidbits. These sentences are an example of such reading. As in driving, where one must stop at the end of each block for a traffic signal, so the start-stop, stop-start jog of too many short sentences wearies the reader.

Most writers, fortunately, are well aware of the importance of *both* long and short sentences, deftly arranged, so that psychological vitality is conserved and variety of verbal surrounding is insured. This artful presentation of thought in appropriate form, including a variety of sentence lengths, is what we call *style* in writing.

The easiest prose to read, therefore, is that which has a varied pace: some sentences short, others long. And at the end of each stand three indications that the thought has finally touched down and momentarily come to rest: a period, a void, and then the capital letter—a towering mass that rises above the skyline of lower case, catching the eye as it runs along the rooftops of the line of print.

The exclamation point. Wham! Following the path of an exclamation point is like following the trail of a bolt from the blue. Your eye plummets from the rooftops of the line of print (along which you normally read) to the base of the word that concludes the exclamatory blast.

The exclamation point stops your reading with a sudden and abrupt jolt. Standing astride the line of print, it literally bars all forward progress.

Momentarily, it crash-lands your attention. It demands that you take time until the statement over which the exclamation point presides registers the full force of its impact upon your mental and emotional consciousness.

Like an emergency brake, the exclamation point is employed with judicious discretion. When it is used, however, it zooms in, directing your reading trajectory to spot zero. It marks the termination of an idea extraordinary. It brings you to a halt before a thought of such exigency that you must award that thought the emotional responsiveness and mental insight which such a thought deserves.

Here is a familiar passage and an excellent example of the use of the exclamation point. Note how it impedes the progress of your reading, grounding the thought time after time, thus giving you an opportunity to appreciate the magnificence of the thought—to contemplate the fullness of the meaning expressed by the words.

Hamlet, the Prince of Denmark, is speaking to his friends:

> "What a piece of work is a man! How noble in reason! how infinite in faculties! in form and moving, how express and admirable! in action, how like an angel! in apprehension, how like a god! the beauty of the world! the paragon of animals!"

The semicolon. On certain avenues, where the traffic lights are adjusted to the flow of traffic, you cruise along approaching a red light. You are prepared to come to a full stop; then, the red flashes green and you have the right of way to proceed.

You find a comparable situation in reading when, cruising down the line of print, your eye encounters a semicolon amid the letters in the line ahead. It means a semi-stop.

Semicolons are employed usually where there are several ideas, complete in themselves, but so closely related to each other that one does not need to come to a complete stop before passing from one idea to another. Usually, all the ideas revolve about some common center of the thought matrix. The semicolon merely indicates the point of transition where the thought shifts to another aspect of the subject under discussion.

Carl Sandburg, for example, was addressing the Joint Session of Congress on the occasion of the sesquicentennial of the birth of Abraham Lincoln. He spoke of Mr. Lincoln as a man "who is both steel and velvet, who is as hard as rock and soft as drifting fog, who holds in his heart and mind the paradox of terrible storm and peace unspeakable and perfect." Then came a description of the events in Lincoln's life during the long, agonizing quadrennium of the war. Note the shifting scene, controlled by semicolons, against the unchanging backdrop of the war:

> During the four years he was President, he at times, especially in the first three months, took to himself the powers of a dictator; he commanded the most powerful armies till then assembled in modern warfare; he enforced conscription of soldiers for the first time in American history; under imperative necessity he abolished the right of *habeas corpus;* he directed politically and spiritually the wild, massive, turbulent forces let loose in civil war.

Signals That Alert You to Conditions Ahead

As certain marks of punctuation demand a full stop, so certain other marks alert the knowledgeable reader to various conditions that await him on ahead. "Forewarned is forearmed" is an aphorism as true in reading as elsewhere; yet the little marks that forewarn the reader are frequently overlooked, except by those who know precisely what to do with a page of print. To see these little marks, on the other hand, and to be sensitive to their message is a mark of the accomplished reader.

The comma. The comma is one of the less pretentious marks on the page—so small, in fact, that many readers never notice it at all. And if you are one of these readers you may need to take special care to see that *for you* the comma does not become lost among the welter of printed words.

To the expert reader, commas are highly informative. They forecast conditions down the printways and tell much concerning conditions on the line ahead.

Commas serve perhaps more purposes in reading than any other single mark. Most marks have only one principal function. The period plainly serves a single purpose: to announce that the reader has arrived at the end of a thought. The exclamation point, likewise, has but one function: to signal the startling or the unusual.

But the comma is different. It may tell you that any one of the following situations exists:

1. that there are two ideas in the sentence, each of which is of about the same degree of importance;
2. that you are faced with a split-level sentence, one that contains two levels of material in terms of degree of importance: the principally important and the secondarily so;
3. that there is a series, a list of items, or an enumeration, the purpose of which array is usually to provide examples to clarify a generalized statement.

We shall now consider each of these uses of the comma separately. For you must learn to recognize on sight a comma usage and to know what to expect, merely because as an expert reader you must be immediately cognizant of the effect of this usage on the thought and meaning of the words which you are reading.

Some commas are known by the company they keep. You may expect to see them always associating with certain words, and when you do it means a sentence with a double idea. Look for a comma preceding any one of five short words:

,and   ,but   ,for   ,or   ,nor

When you see this combination, you may be dead sure that you are looking down a double-barrelled sentence with two main thoughts aimed directly at you. One of these you have just completed by the time you reach the comma-and-word signal; the other is just coming up.

Take, for example, this sentence: He looked at the sentence, and the punctuation helped him to understand its meaning.

Now structure it in this fashion. The double-barrelled ideas connected by the comma-and-word link are readily apparent:

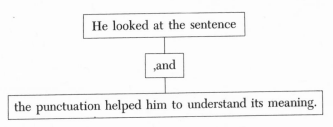

Consider another type of comma usage. It occurs in the split-level sentence. True to its name, the split-level sentence contains two levels of importance of thought: the main idea and the subordinate or subsidiary ideas. The latter are usually separated from the main idea by commas. Commas, therefore, can be highly meaningful in reading. They indicate what is of primary and what is of secondary importance with reference to the main thought. Get the habit, therefore, of noting the comma in the line of print. It will help you to read with skill and precision.

But to return to the split-level sentence. You should learn to recognize this type of sentence the instant you see one. To do so will increase your speed and up your comprehension.

There are, incidentally, two varieties of the split-level sentence. In one, the first few words will alert you. This is the variety in which the incomplete, the subordinate part *precedes* the principal thought, and a comma separates one part from the other. In the second variety of such sentence, the subordinate part is *interpolated among the words* of the main idea. We shall discuss and illustrate each of these varieties separately. In either case, however, the meaning in the subordinate element is always incomplete and sometimes parenthetical.

First, there is the split-level sentence in which the subordinate idea *precedes* the principal thought. Such sentences have a characteristic look. In dummy form, they present a general, overall configurational contour similar to this:

$$\boxed{}, \boxed{}$$

Take the sentence: To read expertly, learn to read the punctuation skillfully. Now, cast that sentence into the general configurational pattern shown above and it will be seen to fit it perfectly:

The main idea, the words that carry the punch of the thought, lie in the latter half of that sentence—after the comma. The part before the comma is a fragment, unresolved, incomplete, dependent upon what follows. It is the latter half that packs the wallop of the thought. Here stand the words that tower in importance over the rest of the sentence. Graphically represented, think of the split-level sen-

tence as a true split *level* in the thought that may very well
be indicated as follows:

So much for the first variety of the split-level sentence. To
spot it, you should eye the introductory words at the beginning of a new sentence. But you should also learn to look for
commas elsewhere. Certain sentences are characterized by
the insertion, *within* the sentence, of two commas separated
by a group of words—and they have a characteristic appearance. These words are usually explanatory phrases of parenthetical "asides." Configurationally, such sentences have this
general appearance:

These "between-the-commas" words, because of their lesser
importance, may be "detoured" if you wish to keep on the
highway of only the main thought. Take, for instance, the
sentence which you are now reading, for this is a good example of a comma-detour-type sentence, and note how, for illustrative purposes, the commas enclose little clusters of words
which could very easily be bypassed and, if this were done,
the thought, as a result, would stand out much more boldly
because no comma-detour obstructions would impede your onward speed along the throughway of the thought.

See that sentence again. It is represented below with the
main line of thought printed in boldface type, the lighter type
face representing the "comma islands" around which an able
reader navigates with ease and adeptness. Try your skill at
verbal navigation:

TAKE,⌐ for instance, └→THE SENTENCE WHICH YOU ARE NOW READING,⌐ for this is a good example of a comma-detour type sentence, └→AND NOTE HOW,⌐ for illustrative purposes, └→THE COMMAS ENCLOSE LITTLE CLUSTERS OF WORDS WHICH COULD VERY EASILY BE BYPASSED AND,⌐ if this were done, └→THE THOUGHT,⌐ as a result, └→WOULD STAND OUT MORE BOLDLY BECAUSE NO COMMA-DETOUR OBSTRUCTIONS WOULD IMPEDE YOUR ONWARD SPEED ALONG THE THROUGHWAY OF THE THOUGHT.

Actually, and this is important in this type of reading, it is not that the reader sees only certain groups of words to the exclusion of others but, rather, that he devotes his *primary* attention only to certain of the more important parts of the sentence. Effective reading is not so much a matter of visual elimination as it is of mental selectivity.

To employ another metaphor, it is almost as though the reader were driving down a busy city thoroughfare. Certain primary matters engage his attention: he studies the traffic before him; he notes vehicles approaching from the rear; he checks the traffic lights; he watches for any pedestrians who may suddenly decide to cross the street. Meanwhile, on the sidewalk an entirely different world of activity is taking place. People are strolling, window shopping, waiting on the corners for the traffic lights to change, standing at a bus stop, and people are moving in opposite directions either up or down the street. He is not oblivious to all this; he simply does not concentrate on it. It is not his primary interest. Let a child, however, dash toward the curb, and he is immediately alert to this detail from the secondary scene. So the skillful reader reads. He concentrates on the main stream of thought traffic; but let a significant subordinate detail be injected, and he notes its presence and is immediately aware of its significance.

Again, and this is particularly true with prose involving long sentences and involved construction, it is sometimes advisable in the interest of speed or of comprehension, in order to clarify the meaning of involved and prolix sentences, to circumvent the comma islands. The skillful reader negotiates them with agility and dexterity, certainly noting their presence in passing, but being neither sidetracked nor impeded by them. You should be able to weave your way in and out, following always the main stream of the thought. Never permit these little comma islands to obstruct your progress down the page or to divert your attention from the pursuit of the main line of the thought.

It is important, therefore, for you to master the detour technique. This can be done only by practice and alertness to the function of the comma in the line of print. We shall have more to say about detouring, however, when we come to the discussion of the colon and the dash as aids in reading.

But back to the comma. It has, finally, one more characteristic appearance in certain sentences. In them, the commas seem to be marching side by side with the words. If we were to represent these sentences in dummy fashion, as we have done with the other types, this kind of sentence might look somewhat like this—with appropriate variations, of course:

In such sentences the comma is used to indicate a series of words, phrases, and clauses; these may be a group of nouns, of adjectives, of verbs, or of phrase or clause units forming a succession of items.

Incidentally, in that last sentence there was a double example of such usage. Were you aware of it?

The colon. The colon is a strange mark to many. They are not quite sure what it means, what its function is, or how to read its message. Yet, of all the signals that forecast oncoming conditions for the reader, the colon is one of the clearest and most unmistakable. Colons alert you to the type of material that lies dead ahead down the roadway of print. They invite you to pass through their slim clearance to a fuller meaning of the statement you have just completed reading.

Now what is the nature of the colon? What does it do?

As a child, I used to delight in proposing conundrums. The urge still persists. Try this one: Why is reading like eating peanuts?

In a little essay by Bennett Cerf entitled, "It's Fun to Read," from the popular Mentor paperback *The Wonderful World of Books*, Mr. Cerf begins one of his paragraphs with the tantalizing statement, "Reading is like eating peanuts," except for the fact that where we have followed the statement with a comma Mr. Cerf followed it with a colon. And *that* is the significant difference.

But, why, you ask, is reading like eating peanuts? What is the common denominator between these two activities? What you need, of course, at this point is an explanation; and the colon that Mr. Cerf inserted following his initial statement alerts you that you are approaching precisely that—an explanation of his first statement.

Have you thought of the answer to the conundrum yet? Why *is* reading like eating peanuts?

Listen to Mr. Cerf.

"Reading is like eating peanuts: once you begin you tend to go on and on."

Of course, you say, I should have thought of that myself. But the point is you needed the colon, and its attendant explanation, to clarify the first part of the statement.

Consider how colons are used. They announce the arrival of an explanation, an enumeration, a direct quotation, a salutation—particularly in a letter, or in the transcription of oral address, and in reference figures. In each instance the progress of the thought is from the broad, generalized statement to the more particularized explanation.

When, for example, you read, "Mr. Lincoln said: . . ." you do not know what Mr. Lincoln said. But follow the colon with the words of the Gettysburg Address and you have explained the general statement in terms of Mr. Lincoln's specific utterance.

Or take another example.

You are reading a mystery novel. The author tells you that the hands of the clock stopped at exactly 4:27. The 27 following the colon indicates the precise minute, amid the sixty possibilities of the hour after 4, to which the hands pointed. The little colon has again fulfilled its function in providing a gateway from the broad and general circle of the hour to the precise and particular moment of that circle around which the hands sweep. That moment is, of course, the twenty-seventh minute.

That is the meaning of 4:27 o'clock.

The dash. Dashes are usually found in pairs. That fact is important for streamlined reading. The dash aids you in negotiating the line of print with the least effort and in bypassing the extraneous and the incidental that obstruct your progress and slow your pace. When they do occur in pairs, dashes serve the same function as parentheses—the material between them is supplementary and, for general comprehension, frequently unessential—and if you are in a big hurry you may sweep around the material within these dashes with a passing glance in much the same manner that a driver swings around a traffic jam in the traffic lane directly ahead of him: he turns into the clear lane and, avoiding obstructions, is off and on his way. Just so, you may expeditiously weave your way down the printed page.

Dashes stand out clearly on the page. Look back into that last paragraph. See how boldly those dashes stand out in the midst of all the surrounding print.

Cultivate an eye for the dash, and you will spot it immediately. If the thought has been entirely comprehensible up to your encounter with the dash, if the explanation or additional comment which lies between the dashes is unnecessary or superfluous, you might detour safely around them—perhaps with a passing glance—as you have probably just done in this sentence.

Both the dash and the colon, then, are signals indicating supplementary or additional information. Sometimes, depending upon your purpose, this information is unnecessary: to have it adds little, if anything, to what you already know. In the interest of expeditious reading, therefore, you might be on the *qui vive* each time you see a dash or encounter a colon. Here may be an opportunity to get ahead in high gear without compromising meaning or becoming unduly encumbered with unnecessary verbiage.

Try this little experiment. Go back, now, to the beginning of this section on "The Dash." Read each sentence again, bypassing all of the material within the dashes or following the colons. See how easily you negotiate the page without anything important being lost.

Here, then, lies one of the secrets of speed in reading: to let the punctuation indicate to you the places which may be safely detoured and to have the knowledge and the skill to do the detouring. This does not mean, of course, that, as with any other type of passing, you should not cast a glance, at least, in the direction of the area that is being bypassed; but if there is no reason for entering it, keep on the highway of the main thought and keep travelling forward.

Generally speaking, dashes might, perhaps, be more safely bypassed than colons. Usually, a more careful glance needs to be directed to the material following the colon. The reason for this is that this material is nearly always a specific example or an illustration of the application of a general principle to a given situation. By its very nature, therefore, such material is sometimes more important in terms of comprehension than a merely parenthetical remark.

The dash, of course, has other uses. These are instances where the dash occurs not in pairs but singly. One of these is the use of the dash to leave you in suspended animation. Usually this usage occurs in a quotation where the speaker stops abruptly and his thought terminates in the elongation of a dash, or where a person does not finish—.

The other instance is the use of the dash before a final statement that summarizes a series of ideas that have preceded the dash.

To summarize, then, to take the place of commas or parentheses, to indicate the interruption of a speaker's words, to mark a sudden break or an abrupt change in the thought, to indicate a final summary of a previous series of ideas—these are the uses of the dash with which every reader should be thoroughly conversant.

Quotation marks. Quotation marks are so distinctly characteristic that they are obvious at first glance. They can mean only two things: (1) someone is speaking, and the material between the quotation marks represents the exact words which he has uttered; (2) a word or phrase is used in an arbitrary or unconventional way.

The knowledgeable reader uses the quotation marks, therefore, to get ahead. Read any page of dialogue. Note how unnecessary—in fact, how banal for the most part—are the comments that accompany the quoted words of a speaker. Take this example (and, following the text, we will insert our own comments):

"Let's go out into the open air," he said. [Of course he *said* it: the quotation marks tell you!]

"I'd rather not," she replied. [What else would you think she was doing except replying?]

"But, I'd like it better," he insisted. [Well, since he's keeping at it, wouldn't you know he's insisting?]

"No, I'm not going!" she snapped. [Sure she did. The exclamation point at the end of her words indicates the snapping point.]

"All right; don't get excited. I'll go out alone," he observed casually. [How else could he have said it, except casually—his words bear all the marks of nonchalance.]

Now, there is a lot of lost motion in all that editorial comment and description by the author. He is telling the reader only what is perfectly obvious through the punctuation and the words themselves.

Let's read it again, this time with all the unnecessary wordage and with all that is perfectly obvious to the sensitive reader deleted. Note how the thought comes through with added clarity.

Ed and Dorothy are speaking. Ed begins by saying:

"Let's go out into the open air."

"I'd rather not."

"But, I'd like it better."

"No, I'm not going!"

"All right; don't get excited. I'll go out alone."

Hemingway writes in such a style. It's a short cut to speed, and it makes the words more lifelike. When you are reading a novel or short story or dialogue, try reading what is *between* the quotation marks only. See, in most cases, how vital and natural—and also meaningful—the dialogue becomes.

The one other use of the quotation marks of interest to the reader is to indicate a word used in an abnormal sense. Take, for instance, the word *bug*. Now, all of us know what a bug is: it's a beetle, an insect. But beetles and bugs can be annoying and irritating. And so when you have been irritated, annoyed, plagued by someone or something you exclaim, Look, now! Don't "bug" me with that any more!

Look!—again

And so, we leave this chapter through the same door by which we entered.

Look!

Look at this page.

What do you see, now?

Print? Paragraphs? Words that affect the flow of the thought?

Punctuation? Ways for getting through with greater speed and less sweat? The unessential and how to circumvent it? Places to use the little tricks that get you through the printed maze pronto?

Yes, all of these.

For, after all, it's what you *see* on a page of print that determines what you do with it. And so, as you see knowingly and respond accordingly, up goes your efficiency.

To bring that efficiency to its peak performance means practice, practice, practice. Every time you pick up a page of print you afford yourself the opportunity to develop your skills to a higher and higher degree.

Keep your eyes open. Next time you are wherever people read—in the library, in the office, on a bus, in a train—observe what those around you are doing. It will not take you long to note how many of them do *not* know what to do with a page of print.

What *you* know now is not, by any means, common knowledge.

Use your knowledge every time you face a page of print. It will pay off handsomely.

Next, let's find out some simple ways that will even further help you to cut your reading time in half.

Before you go on to the next chapter, however, you may want to test your vocabulary and to practice some of the skills you have learned in this one. If so, turn to pages 172 and 174.

3. Cut your reading time in half!

In the jet age, you need to know how to get there—faster! And there are ways of doing it.

As with travel, so with reading. You, Mr. Average Reader, must arrive at your reading destination faster than was necessary for any generation that has ever read before you. You must read faster—much faster indeed—than your father or your grandfather ever did.

Never has there been a day when the pressure of print has been more intense. Everywhere there is something to be read. Business and professional men complain of the drifts of paperwork that engulf their desks; students groan under the weight of textbook assignments and voluminous collateral readings. Everyone, everywhere, must have more facility, more accuracy, more dexterity, more directness in handling the printed word with increased speed and far greater precision.

This chapter will deal with the short cuts to economy with print. It will explore ways of getting more meaning with less struggle. It will suggest ways to cut your reading time in half. It will attempt to show you how to get through the underbrush of verbiage so that you may travel by the shortest and most direct route to your reading destination.

But economy, speed, and directness need imply neither carelessness nor inaccuracy. To advocate dispatch is not to be unmindful that some very critical decisions, some very important operations depend upon the care and accuracy with which one reads; and to equate directness in reading with careless inefficiency is to miss the point entirely.

And yet the idea persists. Two men reveal their apprehension by their remarks. Says one, "My job demands precision and care; I cannot afford to make mistakes merely to gain speed in reading." Another adds, "In my reading, I cannot merely skim the page. Details are important. I must *know* what I read."

Both men are, in fact, basing their statements on strange premises, principally because they do not understand what we mean by speed in reading. Speed they equate with recklessness and irresponsibility. And not infrequently this *is* the equation, as the death toll on our highways eloquently confirms. And so, they regard speed with apprehension and distrust—and well they might. For pure, unbridled, irresponsible speed, whether on the highway or across the level stretches of the printed page, can be hazardous—and its own undoing.

What is open to question, however, are the inferences of the above statements of the two men. Both imply that accuracy must always and of necessity be sacrificed for the sake of speed. Their words seem to suggest that speed and accuracy cannot exist in the company of each other. Yet, strangely enough, the fact of the matter is that frequently the most precise readers are those who get there with greatest expedition—and, in addition, with all their facts aboard.

Research in reading has adequately established that, like a plane taking off from a runway, speed is of prime importance in reading to lift the reader above the level of the verbal symbol into the realm of thought. For, if the reader is to rise above the drag of the printed word, he must develop a certain acceleration which will aid him in soaring into the region where he is unencumbered by the word and is thus free to deal only with the thoughts and the ideas of the author.

This is mature, competent, masterful reading. It is reading at its very best.

To equate such reading with carelessness, therefore, is to have the wrong concept of the function of speed. Speed in reading is the means by which you acquire in the briefest possible time an accurate and precise understanding consistent with your purpose in reading. It has nothing to do with headlong and precipitous recklessness.

Every day those who drive in city traffic are reminded of the fact that speed and care go hand in hand. They negotiate difficult situations with ease and expedition. They get through the vehicular maze with care and safety.

Readers should be no less expert in weaving their way through the avenues of print. Both driver and reader, if they would prove their skill and their ability to cope with the difficult situations which they face, must recognize and observe certain basic principles.

The Basic Principles

1. *Speed depends on purpose.* At the very outset, define the purpose for which you are reading. This will dictate your speed limitations.

Is your aim to get the gist of the article so that you might discuss the principal points and talk about it broadly? Do you wish to know generally what it says, or do you need to have the details of the situation? Is your purpose to see only the general structure and the overall organization of the thought, or do you need to know whether this structure is sufficiently supported by factual detail and substantive evidence?

Whatever your purpose, you should see it clearly and define it accurately in your own mind before you begin to read. The critical question is, What do you want from the page? The clear, concise answer to that question will determine how rapidly it may be wise for you to proceed; it will define the speed limit at which it is safe for you to travel across the page.

2. *Speed depends on knowledge.* The last chapter was entitled "What to Do with a Page of Print." The more you know what to do with the printed page and the more efficiently you apply what you do know, the better you read. Paragraphs should impress you; punctuation should alert you; main ideas should intrude upon your consciousness; details should appear in their proper relationship; the logic of the thought should be clear and unmistakable; the structure of the thought should be obvious to you. And all this should be as second nature. As in driving, certain facts, certain conditions, certain details dictate your approach and your total orientation, so likewise in reading. The knowledgeable reader sees much, and he is—in a very real sense—in the "know" when he glances at a page of print.

3. *Speed is relative and individualistic.* How fast is fast? That all depends.

When America travelled by horse and buggy, the first vehicles that attained a rate of 30 miles an hour were described as travelling at "breakneck" speed. The first train was an awesome sight as it sped down the rails at a top speed of 40 miles per hour. America, then, was not conditioned to travel beyond the jog trot of the horse-and-buggy age. When the air age dawned and heavier-than-air machines attained the frightening rate of 75, 100, and 125 miles per hour, America was stunned by such fantastic speed. Now, the space age is upon us. Astronauts encircle the earth in an hour and a half and will voyage to the moon at cruising speeds of 20,000 miles per hour!

How fast is fast? Speed is relative.

If you are now reading at 200 words per minute—which is

average for many readers—and you increase your rate to 300 words per minute with equal comprehension, you have upped your reading rate by 50 per cent, and you should take justifiable pride in your achievement. While the expert reader may cruise along at 600 words per minute, and by comparison you may feel greatly inferior to him as you trudge along at one-third of his jet-stream pace, yet you should remember that to equal your gain he would have to increase his pace from 600 to 900 words per minute. Thus, speed in reading is an individual matter and improvement is relative. When *your* reading curve starts upward, you are on your way. Only one thing matters then—to keep going!

4. *Speed depends upon mental agility.* You should recognize certain facts with respect to reading generally and to your own reading in particular, and they are facts which cannot be ignored. Speed in reading depends in part upon speed in thinking. As some of us are physically more nimble than others; so, likewise, some of us are more agile mentally than others. This is merely one of the facts of life.

The act of reading demands that the reader be intellectually keen and mentally alert to each expressed idea or implied meaning on the printed page. Many factors condition this mental agility. Your word-hoard must be ample, and you must be able to associate a word with its precise meaning instanter. Also, you must read not only by single words but by groups of words; and from these groups should arise "islands of thought"—meaningful phrases—which, in turn, combine to create that more fantastic complex of meaning which we have, for the want of a better term, called "comprehension."

Insofar as the individual is receptive to the ideas of others, open-minded and attentive to the message of the page, and intellectually active and inquiring with respect to the validity or logic of the ideas expressed, he is just so much the better equipped thereby to increase his speed and improve his comprehension.

5. *Speed is upped by experience.* The more you know— the more experience you have—the better you read. For, reading touches many areas of one's life and thought. We live vicariously through the pages of a book.

In a very real sense, your reading is you: all that you are, all that you have experienced, all that you have learned. Bring to the page a broad background of experience or a wide spectrum of knowledge, or a deep appreciation of life, and you are at home with ideas from many different sectors of human activity, from many angles of human thought. This orientation places you in a more advantageous position as a reader, because by means of it you can synthesize your knowledge and experience so that you may relate meanings more quickly to what you already know and thus apprehend the thought of the author with greater ease and facility.

6. *Speed is not guaranteed by gadgetry.* Gadgets, such as reading pacers, visual perceptive devices, and other "reading machines" may not of themselves increase your reading rate or improve your comprehension. Do not be taken in by advertisements that claim such instruments to be absolutely necessary for reading improvement. They may help you; again, they may not. No one can say categorically.

Generally, such aids are little more than mechanical motivators which hurry you along, ever faster and faster. Shutters descend, closing off the page so that you cannot regress and waste your time rereading. Again, beams of light glide down the page, challenging you to race along with them so that you cover the page more quickly. These devices discourage dawdling along the printways. They spur you forward. They demand that you concentrate—and read.

At best, however, they are but artificial ways of getting the task done. Reading speed should come from *within* the individual. It cannot be superimposed; nor can you go around, from this day forward, toting a pacer or other cumbersome device whenever you wish to read.

As we have seen to this point in the discussion, reading is a complex of many factors, only one of which is speed—which is itself complex and dependent upon still other elements. Speed is acceleration, plus understanding, plus a comprehensive grasp of the blueprint of the author's thought; and all these intensified by your own mental agility, intellectual awareness, and associative vitality.

Speed can be upped. The time you spend in getting meaning from the page can be pared down.

Certain practical pointers may aid you materially in saving both time and effort as you read. They may perhaps help you to cut your reading time in half without sacrificing either your comprehension or losing any of your total reading power. In fact, both should be improved.

Here, then, are the pointers.

Practical Pointers for Cutting Your Reading Time in Half

1. *Faster reading begins at your finger tips.* The most versatile gadget for aiding reading speed was built into you before you were born—your index finger. Rightly used, it can assist you in getting more information from the printed page than any other aid.

One of the marks of an expert reader is the ease with which he flips. This is really not as terrifying as it sounds, for every effective reader flips often; and, in fact, it must become a habit with you if you would learn to read really well.

The first law of the printed page is this: Before doing anything else, use your index finger to flip through the pages of a book, a chapter, an article you intend to read.

Did you flip through *this* chapter before you began to read it? Check your answer to that question here: ☐ Yes ☐ No.

If you checked "Yes," go to the second of the practical pointers in this section; if "No," then let's flip now.

Do it this way: Hold the book with your left hand supporting the open pages. Turn back to the beginning of the chapter. With your right index finger, beginning at the upper right-hand corner, flip each right-hand page.

As you flip—look! What do you see?

Had you given this chapter this high-speed approach earlier, you would have seen in the first ten seconds of your reading the whole outline of the thought. From a skeletal standpoint, the chapter looks like this:

CUT YOUR READING TIME IN HALF!

I. The basic principles
   A. Speed depends on purpose.
   B. Speed depends on knowledge.
   C. Speed is relative and individualistic.
   D. Speed depends upon mental agility.
   E. Speed is upped by experience.
   F. Speed is not guaranteed by gadgetry.
II. Practical pointers for cutting your reading time in half
   A. Faster reading begins at your finger tips.
   B. Read only the main ideas.
   C. Know when you've had enough.
   D. Read only the essential words.
   E. Read the graphics.
   F. Beat the fact to the finish line.

Now, having merely flipped and looked, you already have a head start for reading the chapter in more detail. Looking at a relief map or out of the window of a plane aids you in seeing the whole terrain more clearly. The country always looks different from the upstairs vantage point, and so you travel with a more comprehensive and knowledgeable view. The same is true with the reading landscape. Regard it first from upstairs. See it from up there, and you will see how the verbal land lies. You will discern outline, organization, relationships of rank and importance, and structure in the body of the thought that will make your reading much more meaningful.

Author, editor, typesetter, design and format personnel have all joined forces in the making of a book. All this effort has been expended for one purpose only: to facilitate your reading, to speed you on your way by making the book more easily comprehended in a shorter time and with minimal effort.

Such is the cooperation that aims to speed your reading— and it begins at your finger tips.

> RULE 1: *Never attempt to read anything without first doing the flip. Let your index finger discover the structure and the master outline of the thought.*

2. *Read only the main ideas.* Strike for the bull's eye. Aim for the main thought.

Earlier in these pages we discussed the structure of the normal paragraph and pointed out that it followed largely the behavior patterns of the human thought processes. In most paragraphs, therefore, the main idea will be stated first. (For a review of this discussion see pages 30–33.)

Try this technique: Read only the first sentence of each paragraph down the page. If the sentences thus read consecutively make sense, keep going. So long as the sense keeps coming in, you keep rolling down the page.

Have you been reading the chapter this way? ☐ Yes ☐ No.

If "Yes," go on to the next pointer; if "No," turn back to the beginning of the chapter and read the first sentence at the beginning of each paragraph successively.

Just to get you started, here is what you will find:

> In this jet age, you need to know how to get there—
> faster! As with travel, so with reading. Never has there been
> a day when the pressure of print has been more intense.
> This chapter will deal with the short cuts to economy with
> print. But economy, speed, and directness need imply neither
> carelessness nor inaccuracy. . . .

And so, main idea after main idea, the thought spreads out—lucidly, meaningfully, logically. You have now more than the mere skeletonization of the thought outline. You have added the next deeper level of meaning. You have, in fact, a brief summary of what the chapter is all about.

But what to do if the thought sequence breaks? When a break in the flow of the thought does occur, it usually indicates that the last sentence of the *preceding* paragraph is important for thought continuity. Try, therefore, in such instances, reading the last sentence of the preceding paragraph. Usually, you will find that the hiatus disappears and that the thought flows smoothly again.

> RULE 2: *Try reading only the first sentence of each paragraph. Keep going so long as the thought flows smoothly and logically. In case of a break or gap in the thought, read the last sentence of the preceding paragraph, thus repairing the break; then, resume your first-sentence-only pace.*

3. *Know when you've had enough.* Do not read needlessly. Determine exactly what you want from the page before you. Then, read to get it.

By employing the first two pointers, already discussed, you should have obtained in the shortest possible time (1) an outline of the thought and (2) the sequence of the main ideas. Now, take account of stock. Is this *all* you want? Then, quit while you're ahead; and get on to other things.

Constantly, however, you will need to appraise what the

page is giving you: Is it sufficient for your reading needs or do you require still more? Perhaps you must have additional information; you need specific facts and supporting details. If so, for a pointer on how to get these data in the most direct way refer back to the discussion earlier in this book on reading a paragraph for maximum awareness of the thought. (See pages 48–50.)

> RULE 3: *Define in your own mind, clearly and precisely, your purpose for reading and exactly how far you need to delve into the material being read.*

4. *Read only the necessary words.* Contrary to the popular belief, not every word on the page is essential in order to understand what the author is saying. Actually, you could do with less than half the words the author wrote and still get the thought clearly.

Try this. Read a page as you might telegraph a message: maximum of meaning crammed into minimal wordage. This is telegraphic reading. With a little practice, you can learn to read telegraphically. For example, the 103 words in this paragraph might be compressed to 36 with no loss of thought, as in the example following:

TELEGRAPHIC VERSION

NOT EVERY WORD NECESSARY TO UNDERSTAND AUTHOR. YOU COULD DO WITH LESS THAN HALF. READ AS YOU TELEGRAPH—MAXIMUM THOUGHT, MINIMAL WORDS. PRACTICE. PARAGRAPH OF 103 WORDS MIGHT BE COMPRESSED TO 36 WITH NOTHING LOST.

What does reading like this mean? It means a tremendous surge in reading power! It means that you have increased the economy of your reading 286 per cent. It means that if you read this book, which contains about 50,000 words, by the telegraphic method, reducing it by the same proportion that the paragraph above was reduced, it would shrivel to a mere 17,500 words.

Think of it still another way. If you are reading at only 250 words per minute, by keeping the same pace and by reading only the essential words of the text, you would actually boost your rate to 715 words per minute!

How is telegraphic reading done? The magic key word is *practice*. Because of early learning patterns established in the elementary grades, most of us are conditioned to read every single word. For many of us it is a lifelong habit. Consciously, therefore, this habit must be broken and a new approach to the page established.

Practice in this manner: let your eyes run along the line of print, always looking for meaning, and let your eyes pick up whatever words they can grasp. Do not be disturbed if, during the first several practice periods, you feel that you are skidding down the line without establishing much traction with the thought. More and more your mind will become selective. Your eyes *see* all the words, but you will teach your mind to receive and dwell upon those only which are essential for conveying the meaning. After a while you will look at a page and see only those relatively few words on it which are necessary for the reading of it.

Do not be discouraged, however, if the first few attempts are unrewarding. Habits are never easily broken, and you cannot expect to undo in a few fleeting moments of practice what you have been strengthening and reinforcing over the years.

RULE 4: *Practice telegraphic reading. Read only the essential words necessary for conveying the thought.*

5. *Read the graphics.* The Chinese had a proverb. It was to the effect that one picture was worth ten thousand words.

Now, that may be stretching it—slightly. Nevertheless, it does point to an important fact that many readers overlook; and it does suggest a short cut to your reading destination.

Many readers disregard the graphics. They fail to see the pictures, the illustrations, the maps, the graphs, the charts, the sectional drawings, and other types of graphic presentation. And if they notice them at all, they see them only peripherally and marginally.

The message of the graphic is usually presented twice: once in the graphic itself, again in the text accompanying the illustration.

Most readers belabor the text first. They struggle through the verbal explanation, sometimes referring to the graphic as they read, at other times disregarding it altogether.

This is to attack the situation in reverse. Perhaps a more efficient way would be to attack the graphic head on, and then, where it is not self-evident or clear, to consult the text.

Usually the graphic conveys its message at a glance; the verbal explanation is slower and more time-consuming. Yet, even in spite of this, many readers invariably elect to take the longer and more tedious route.

RULE 5: *Read the graphics. Many graphics may be grasped at a glance. With those that are self-evident, skip the verbal explanation and get on with your reading.*

6. *Beat the fact to the finish line.* In a new paragraph, be alert to the first sentence of the author. For, in his first few words, he at times shows his whole hand. Having uttered his first sentence, he frequently has said all. Then, there is nothing left but a fooling around. And so, the author has, in consequence, little choice but to belabor an already-stated thought, to repeat an idea, or to engage in mere sound and fury signifying little more than nothing.

For an example of this type of writing, take the sentence: "Many readers disregard the graphics."

Now, what else is there to say? If readers disregard the graphics, then—they disregard the graphics. That's it! That's all there is to it. It is the truth, the whole truth, and little more is left to say about that truth. Actually, what *is* left to say, if anything? Once having uttered this all-inclusive statement, how would an author proceed should he wish to develop a paragraph from it?

Would you like to know? Then, turn back to the second paragraph in the preceding section, dealing with the fifth of the practical pointers for cutting your reading time in half. (Page 83, paragraph 1.)

Note how the paragraph proceeds. It states the main idea. The rest of the paragraph adds exactly nothing to that main idea. To spend much time on such writing is to be wasting time. I hope, when you read it originally, you gave it short shrift. It deserves no better fate!

Expert readers recognize such paragraphs the moment they see them; and, when they encounter one in their reading, they make sure to beat the author to his own finish line. They leap to the final period of the paragraph without becoming entangled in matter of no value.

But aside from leaping over the whole flatland of inconsequential words, there is still another way to beat the fact to the finish line: become a kangaroo reader.

Many paragraphs provide an opportunity for kangaroo reading. You can get through them with literally a hop, a hop, and a hop! Moreover, such paragraphs usually cue the reader that such kangaroo behavior in reading is possible. They begin characteristically: "There are three principal causes for poor reading. The first of these is . . . ." At this point, you note "the first" cause; and, if you are agile, you glide through the first cause with maximum speed and the greatest of ease. Then, your eye is open for "the second is . . ."; and that cause is dispatched with equal celerity; now, "finally . . . ," and that is the signal for the last jump. Just beyond looms the end of the paragraph. You literally hop from cause to cause by following the cues given you along the way.

In reading such paragraphs, however, you must take the initiative. The paragraph will cue you, but you must seek out the meaning. You must leap from fact to fact and, thus, beat the author to the finish line.

> RULE 6: *Read no more than you must to get the thought; look for cues which will aid you to beat the fact to the finish line.*

Practice!

And so, with these six hints for faster, more efficient reading, you should be able to cut your reading time in half. You will perhaps want to employ a battery of techniques in any given reading situation. For that reason, you should become thoroughly conversant with them and their use, not only by reading about them but by putting these suggestions to the pragmatic test again and again whenever you face the printed page.

Improvement in reading cannot be a static matter, carried on inertly in a vacuum. You cannot effect any improvement merely by reading about it in a book like this. Equally impossible is learning to swim by being comfortably ensconced in an easy chair and reading a book about it. If you want to learn to swim, you must dive into the water. Likewise, if you wish to improve your reading, you must dive into print and actively apply the advice in the book to printed page after printed page. Soon you will find that your reading skills are improving and that you are on your way toward cutting your reading time in half.

Now, you have come just about to the mid-point in this discussion of what to do with the page of print. By this time, you should be forming some habits that will help you to expedite your reading skills and advance your progress. By this time you should be beginning to understand the rationale of the printed word: that pages are not merely filled with drifts of print, but that to the discerning mind and the seeing eye all is orderly and rational, planned so by an author that a reader may reach his destination more quickly and effortlessly. But a great deal depends upon the habits which you are forming as a basic foundation of your program for reading improvement. How commonly have you made these important habits your instinctive reactions when you come into the presence of print?

Turn to page 175. There you will find a self-evaluation test. It should serve two purposes: one, to provide you a quick review of the important points and procedures discussed during this part of the book; two, to give you an opportunity to appraise honestly your reading habit growth and to see your remaining needs in planning for further improvement.

4. Keeping up
with the news

Every day 95 million Americans read the newspaper.

Let a newspaper or printer's strike happen to one of our great dailies, and everyone feels the impact. At once, we are amazingly aware of our dependence on the daily paper. We are, in a very real sense, a nation of newspaper readers.

And the modern newspaper is a liberal education in itself. It can test the range of your awareness and interest in the marvellously complex contemporary world. The late William Lyons Phelps, literary critic, author, and educator, remarked on one occasion that the newspaper is an accurate gauge of one's contact with life, adding that every person ought to find something of interest on every page of the daily paper.

What a test!

Think of the wide appeal that an edition has—the broad horizon of human interest it covers: the history-making events of each day; the editorial thought interpreting those events; the doings of our fellow men, citizens and neighbors; fashions; gardens and gardening; art, both static and performing; crossword puzzles and cartoons; hobbies—coin and stamp collecting; sports; radio and record listening; home-improvement projects; the business world and stock reports; education; travel; books; and the never-never-land of television and the theater. Add to this the lost-and-found and classified columns, the obituaries, and the advice to the lovelorn and troubled; and you have a wide spectrum of human life and a broad range of human interest.

Why not take your pencil and check on page 179 those features of the newspaper which you read *regularly?* It will give you some indication of your general alertness to life and your awareness of the world around you. After you have checked your newspaper-reading habits in the inventory list, count the number of items you have checked. Evaluate your general-interest score as follows: 20 to 25 items checked indicates your interest and readership index is excellent; 15 to 19 items checked indicates it is good; 10 to 14 items, acceptable; if only 5 to 9 items, it is poor; and if below 5 items, you are muffing your daily opportunity to wake up, live, and be interesting. How's your readership and interest index? Check it here: __ excellent, __ good, __ acceptable, __ poor, __ get going fast!

So, then, here is the first suggestion for keeping up with the news: Enlarge your personal coverage; read more features and departments of the newspaper than you now do. Make it a habit to add one additional department to your reading each week in addition to those you now read regularly. It will up your general-interest index in the life and world around you.

The New York Times has an engaging slogan for its readership advertisements: "Read *The New York Times;* it is more interesting—and you will be too!" This is effective advertising, but it is also valuable self-improvement advice. Vivacious, interesting, alert, knowledgeable people are those who keep up with the news and happenings in the world. They are interested in the doings and affairs of life about them.

Personal improvement lies as close as your daily newspaper. Not only is the newspaper a vital force in heightening the power of personal effectiveness, but the role of the newspaper is indispensable in the life of a nation.

Listen to Thomas Jefferson, author of the Declaration of Independence, on the subject of the importance of newspapers. The time is the days of the creation of the early Republic. His words are daring and revolutionary. He is writing to Colonel Edward Carrington, January 16, 1787:

> The basis of our government being the opinion of the people, the very first object should be to keep that right; and were it left to me to decide whether we should have a government without newspapers, or newspapers without a government, I should not hesitate a moment to prefer the latter. But I should mean that every man should receive those papers and be capable of reading them.

And so, since newspapers are so important, not only to the personal life of each citizen, but also in the life of the entire nation, you should appreciate their importance and have a master plan for attacking the daily paper. Here is a suggested guide by one of the nation's great dailies.

Get Your Reading Down to a Schedule

Get your newspaper reading down to a daily schedule. With proper planning, there is no reason why you cannot get through the entire paper each day, no matter how crowded that day may be. Dr. Charles Eliot, erstwhile president of Harvard University, popularized the 5-foot shelf of Harvard Classics by claiming that a man, if he so wished, might gain a liberal education by spending just fifteen minutes a day with the great books of mankind.

The *New York Herald Tribune* published some time ago as an educational service to its readers a little booklet entitled *How to Get the Most Out of Your Newspaper*. One of the preliminary remarks is that a newspaper is no formal dinner . . . "It's a read-as-you-please buffet of news, interpretation, specialized information, entertainment and advertising, freshly prepared each day. You can nibble or feast, according to your appetite."

In a section entitled "To Have and to Fold," the *Tribune* suggests that the standard-size eight-column paper (for which nobody has yet found a substitute) measures slightly under a yard when opened and laid out flat. "That's pretty broad in the beam," comments the *Tribune* writer, and "for people who handle their standard-size newspapers as if they were hanging up the week's wash, there is a simple tidy way to move through a large city paper with no more effort than you would expend on a pocket magazine." Here's how:

Step 1: Open the paper and fold it in half, lengthwise. Since a newspaper has eight columns, this gives you a reading area of four columns.

Step 2: Front page—start reading on the right side, where most of the important stories of the day are usually placed. When finished, turn over to the left-hand half of the page.

Step 3: To continue on into the paper, fold back the front page, thus exposing the first four columns of page 2. By folding the entire page back into the paper, you uncover the right-hand half of page 2 and the left-hand half of page 3.

Step 4: After you have read pages 2 and 3 in book fashion, as you read page 1, fold in these pages and proceed through the entire paper.

Read as you will, but *read!* And, if you are to make your reading time count, you should get your time that you spend with each day's paper down to a systematic attack on the day's news.

Take a half-hour, and fit your time spent with the newspaper into this thirty-minute period somewhat according to the following suggested schedule:

1. *The Bird's-Eye View.* (3 minutes). Get a comprehensive idea of the paper's content for the day. Skim the headlines; glance at the index. This is the menu of goodies which the paper for that day offers. Note what seems to be especially attractive reading. Read the headlines and subheads of the top news stories of the first several pages. All this can be compressed into three minutes.

2. *The Day's Big News* (12 minutes). Big news means those important happenings which are noteworthy at three distinct and important levels: local, national, and international. As you read try to see the world in one piece and the news at each level as a part of a larger and overall trend of the times. This will help you to integrate your thinking; it will help to make you comprehensive in your life-and-world view. In the "big news" do not overlook the newspaper advertising. The "ads" may be for you some of the biggest news of the day: good news for your pocketbook and welcome news for the household budget! You'll probably want to do your armchair shopping during your first fifteen minutes with your newspaper. More will be said about the skills needed in reading these advertisements in a later chapter of this book.

3. *What Does It All Mean?* (5 minutes). There's a take-over in Uganda, a revolution in Mozambique, an insurrection in Lilliput, and a cargo of green cheese newly arrived from the moon. All top news. What do these events mean? To unravel the significance of such news, to set events in their proper perspective, to help you form your own opinions about the happenings of the world of today and to see their implications for the world of tomorrow, you need the comment of skilled interpreters. And so, you read the columnists. It is their job to give the world's affairs their proper significance as they see it.

Then, there is the newspaper's own interpretation with respect to these events. For it, you turn to the editorial page, where the newspaper takes its own stand on the major issues of the day.

Then, also, there are the readers who, like yourself, have a chance to express their own views of the news in the "Letters to the Editor" column. All in all, many opportunities are available by means of which you may assess the essential meaning and implications of the events that are taking place on the world stage and before the news footlights.

4. *Taken to Taste* (10 minutes). Here is the final one-third of your half-hour. This block of time you may spend as you wish on your interests and for your own enjoyment. Your final time parcel may be devoted to the sports pages, the women's pages, the financial section, society, book, or travel columns, the classifieds or the comics. Here is your chance to enjoy the salmagundi of leftovers not preempted by the previous reading schedule. Strive, however, to make your news reading a well-balanced meal; so doing will give you a sharper, fairer picture of what is happening in the world each day, rather than in just your own province of special interest.

And so, like any other reading activity, newspaper reading is a habit. Like all habits, it must be established through regular practice and a daily routine. Set aside a certain time each day; and then, allow nothing to deter you from following your predetermined schedule. Follow the plan and time scheme outlined above. It will help you to form the habit of reading the newspaper regularly and systematically. Soon you will find that you are keeping up with the news.

But to read a newspaper intelligently, you should also know something about the structure of the writing which the paper contains. Most of the writing in the newspaper can be divided into two general types: news reporting and editorial reaction.

Each of these is a discrete style of writing and demands to be read in the light of its own peculiar structural characteristics.

How to Read the News

Let us consider first how to read a news item.

As every reporter knows, the news story has its own distinctive style and special structural form. Here, for example, is a news story in miniature:

FIRE DESTROYS EMPIRE RUBBER PLANT

CENTERVILLE, March 5. — A fire, of reportedly incendiary origin, swept through the Empire Tire and Rubber Company plant last night, causing an estimated million dollars damage.

According to Fire Chief Smith, the fire was discovered after midnight by a night watchman. The blaze brought four-alarm fire-fighting equipment from all parts of the city. The flames, apparently fed by quantities of benzene in the processing division, raged out of control for four hours.

E. B. Strongheart, president of the firm, said last night that he felt sure that after a full appraisal of the loss, the firm would rebuild immediately.

Empire was one of the oldest rubber-processing plants in the area. It has been in Centerville since 1892.

Suppose we take this same news story and rearrange it in the form of an inverted pyramid or big wedge. The base of the pyramid is the area of greatest compression of fact; and, inverted, it becomes the first paragraph of the story. Here the basic news elements of the story are found; for the first paragraph is the place where the reader finds the essential questions answered: Who? When? Where? What? Why and/or how?

Below is an analysis of the news story in schematic and analytical form:

FIRE DESTROYS EMPIRE RUBBER PLANT

Basic
elements:
the story in
miniature

CENTERVILLE, March 5.— A fire, of reportedly incendiary origin, swept through the Empire Tire and Rubber Company plant last night, causing an estimated million dollars damage.

Who?[1]
How?
Where?
When?

What?

Added details
of secondary
importance

According to Fire Chief Smith, the fire was discovered after midnight by a night watchman. The blaze brought four-alarm fire-fighting equipment from all parts of the city. The flames, apparently fed by quantities of benzene in the processing division, raged out of control for four hours.

Nothing directly
relating to the
fire; rather, the
follow-up plans

E. B. Strongheart, president of the firm, said last night that he felt sure that, after a full appraisal of the loss, the firm would rebuild immediately.

Nothing to do with
the fire; instead,
the history of the
company

Empire was one of the oldest rubber-processing plants in the area. It has been in Centerville since 1892.

[1]The fire is considered the principal actor in this story.

Now, look closely at the analytical version of the news story. Study it. Each paragraph tells you something relative to the Empire Tire and Rubber Company; yet each paragraph strays further and further from the causal event that really made the news—the fire itself.

The story-in-miniature is given in the first paragraph. Here is where you get the wrong-end-of-the-telescope view of the news. The account of the fire is complete, but compact.

The next paragraph zooms in to give you certain details of the fire in clearer perspective.

Then paragraphs three and four veer away from the account of the fire itself. Paragraph three looks to the future, toward the appraisal of the loss and the rebuilding of the plant; paragraph four, on the other hand, looks to the past, recounting in brief the long history of the plant and giving the date of its origin.

And so, the second suggestion for keeping abreast of the news is to keep alert to what the news story is saying—precisely—and what the journalist is doing paragraph by paragraph down the column.

How Accurate Is Your Newspaper Reading?

You've heard it said that you can't believe a word of anything you read in the newspapers? Of course, you have. The statement is commonplace. But is it true?

An event happens. The papers report it. You read about it. Then, you talk with a friend who was at the scene and actually saw it happen. He tells you an entirely different version from what you have read. And so, you cry out, "I knew it; you can't believe a thing you read in the papers!"

There is inaccuracy and discrepancy in news reporting—no doubt of that. Somewhere, somehow the communication lines have become snarled. But is the snarl at the reading or the writing end of the news-reporting process? Let's attempt to find out.

If you wish to review the news account of the fire, do it now. Then, turn to page 180. There you will find a test to evaluate your skills in newspaper reading. Take the test; but after you turn to page 180, do not refer back to the news story.

What Did the Test Reveal?

Now that you have taken the test and checked the accuracy of your answers, what did the test reveal to you?

To find the answer to this question, let's look at some of the aims and purposes behind the test. First of all, the test was an opportunity for you to assess such a common ability as accuracy and precision in reading simple, everyday prose and comprehending exactly what it said. The test probed into such questions as these: Do you know precisely what you have read? Have you grasped the thought of the author exactly as he has presented it? These are basic questions for which every reader should have immediate and unequivocal answers. What did the test reveal about these matters with respect to your reading?

If, perhaps, you were not as accurate in your reading as you could have been—if, for example, you did not distinguish as clearly as perhaps you should have done between hearsay and happening, between rumor and fact—the test might suggest that each time you pick up a daily paper you are granted the opportunity to enhance the skills of accuracy and precision and to increase your complete awareness of what the writer is saying. Such skills, if carefully developed, will pay large dividends as they become a habitual part of your total reading behavior.

Was there less fact and more opinion in the article than you recognized before taking the test? Many readers do not always keenly separate fact and opinion; and yet, until the awareness of this need is brought clearly to their attention by an experience such as was provided by the test, they do not recognize need for improvement in this area of their reading efficiency. In this respect, what did the test reveal to you?

To increase your awareness in distinguishing between what is stated categorically as fact and what is opined as true, try this interesting experiment. Take any issue of a daily paper and encircle each word, every phrase, each expression that indicates that a categorical statement of fact has *not* been made. You may be astonished at the frequency with which responsibility for a statement is shifted to another's shoulders or attributed to an impersonal source. Such expressions as "allegedly," "apparently," "it was estimated that," "according to reports," "observers on the scene noted that," and similar phraseology lurk in abundance in the dusky, narrow corridors of the newspaper printways.

Here, for example, is an account of tragedy on the high seas. Let us do with it exactly as we have just recommended. All ascriptive phrases have been encircled. In addition, let's see how a wide-awake, alert reader would react to this story. What thoughts would flash through his mind? What questions would he ask as he reads?

The news story below, except for some shortening, is exactly the account of a fire at sea as it was printed in *The* [Washington, D.C.] *Evening Star* on the day of the disaster. The story itself occupies the left-hand column. The right-hand column contains the asides, the observations, the reactions, and the silent comments of a competent and alert reader as he reads the story, paragraph by paragraph.

Luxury Liner Burns

Fate of 135 Unsure as Fire Rages Off Cuba

German Freighter Picks Up Survivors; All in Good Shape

MIAMI, Fla. (AP)—A raging fire engulfed the cruise ship Viking Princess off the eastern tip of Cuba today and its passengers and most of the crew abandoned it to the sea. [1]

The coast guard said 362 of an estimated 495 persons aboard the Miami-based luxury liner were plucked from the Atlantic by a German freighter, the Cap Nort. [2]

1. Here is the lead paragraph:
   WHO? "A raging fire." WHEN? "Today" WHERE? "Off the eastern tip of Cuba." WHAT? It engulfed the *Viking Princess.* HOW? So much that the passengers and most of the crew abandoned it.

2. Obviously the Coast Guard (an organization) cannot "say." A closer-to-fact statement would be: Lieutenant Blank, a spokesman for the Coast Guard said. . . . Note also a discrepancy between the headline and the arithmetic in the paragraph: 495 minus 362 equals 133. Headline says 135!

[3] "All are in good shape," a Coast Guard spokesman said. "We have not been able to determine whether there are any casualties.

[4] "Flames are engulfing the superstructure."

[5] At Norfolk, Va., U.S. Atlantic Fleet headquarters said the Viking Princess carried 235 passengers and 260 crew members.

[6] That left 135 persons unaccounted for, but a navy spokesman said they may have been crewmen left aboard "presumably to fight the fire."

[7] Arthur Crane, vice president of the booking agency for the ship in Miami, estimated the number of crew members at 250. He confirmed that the princess carried 235 passengers.

Under Veteran Skipper

[8] It was under the command of Capt. Otto Thoresen, a veteran of 30 years at sea.

[9] Two U.S. Navy destroyers, the USS Wilkenson and Owens, were reported on the scene by Atlantic Fleet headquarters and three other ships were en route.

[10] Fire struck the 536-foot motor ship as it was sailing north through the Windward Passage, about midway between Cuba and Haiti.

3. Still Coast Guard reporting: "All are in good shape." Meaning what? No deformed ones among them! or none is ill nor injured? Recognize this as colloquial jargon.

4. Seems like a *non sequitur.* Is this a "because" statement? Can't determine casualties *because* flames are engulfing superstructure. If not this, then what?

5. Another agency is heard from: U.S. Atlantic Fleet Hqrs. Their total of persons aboard checks with that of the Coast Guard.

6. Who is this Navy spokesman? Presumably he is from U.S. Atl. Fleet Hqrs. The statement, however, is meaningless: "*That* left . . ." What left? You cannot possibly derive 135 from the figures in the previous paragraph.

7. This is the third agency to be heard from so far. Note the discrepancy between the Crane estimate and the fleet headquarters estimate with respect to the number of men in the crew. There is a ten-man difference. (See paragraph 5.) The passenger figures agree.

8. Who made this statement about the skipper: the newspaper, the Coast Guard, fleet headquarters, or Crane? What is the purpose of it? What has it to do with the fire? Why insert it here?

9. Let's keep track of the arithmetic. "On the scene" were the *Owens,* the *Wilkenson,* and the *Cap Nort;* three others were "en route." Three there; three coming. Check this figure against paragraph 13!

10. This paragraph intrudes. It splits the account of the rescue ships. At this point it is out of place. Perhaps it might more logically go between paragraphs 14 and 15.

"The only ship we have talked to is the Cap Nort," a Coast Guard spokesman said in Miami. "The only message we received was 'fire in the engine room. All stations stand by.'" [11]

About five hours after the first distress call, a Navy plane flying over the scene reported to the Coast Guard that the fire appeared to be raging out of control. [12]

4 Ships Close By

"The aircraft said there were four ships in the vicinity of the Viking Princess as well as six life boats," said the Coast Guard spokesman. [13]

The Coast Guard said it did not know if all aboard the liner had been evacuated, but the booking agency spokesman said there apparently was no loss of life. [14]

The initial report of trouble was received by the Coast Guard in Miami at 1:44 a.m. It first identified the ship as the Viking Princess, but later said it was the Liberian freighter Navigator. [15]

Then the Coast Guard determined the fire actually was aboard the Princess. Difficulty in making radio contact with shipping in the area apparently led to the confusion. [16]

En route to the scene were the destroyer escort USS Brumby, the minesweeper USS Swerve, both from Guantanamo, Cuba, and the Coast Guard cutter Cook Inlet, which was on patrol in the area. [17]

The navy said the Wilkenson, from Newport, R.I., and the Owens, from Norfolk, were training at the U.S. base at Guantanamo and diverted to the scene. [18]

Had Luxurious Features

The viking princess boasted 100 per cent air-conditioning, two outdoor tiled swimming pools, a 275-seat theater, and plush dining facilities. [19]

It has a total of 228 cabins on five decks providing accommodations for a possible 627 passengers. Each cabin has a private bath. [20]

The 16-year-old ship has a displacement of 17,600 tons, a length of 536 feet and a 64-foot beam. Its twin screws are driven by diesel engines. [21]

The Viking Princess is of Norwegian registry and manned by a predominantly Norwegian crew. It is operated by the Flagship Line Agency, Inc., sales agent for Berge Sigval Bergesen of Oslo, Norway. [22]

11. How, then, did the Coast Guard get all the figures in paragraph 2 if the *only* message received was this one. The *only* message reported "flames in the engine room," yet paragraph 3 has the Coast Guard reporting "flames engulfing the superstructure."

12. A fourth source of information. Still nothing which would give Coast Guard information on the number aboard, yet see paragraph 3.

13. What's up? Again, the arithmetic does not check! Paragraph 9: three on the scene; three coming. Yet, the aircraft (Navy) saw four. Might one have been the vanguard of the three that were coming?

14. The chaos that always accompanies an emergency is written large across this paragraph and the ones that follow. As elsewhere in this story, reports conflict, identity is mistaken, confusion is present in paragraphs 14, 15, 16.

15. 16. Confusion! Confusion!

17. This is an amplification of paragraph 9 and from a reading standpoint belongs with it. The story now begins to lose altitude rapidly. From here on we get incidental information that is only collaterally related to the principal disaster.

18. 19. 20. 21. 22. These paragraphs diverge from the account of the disaster to give supplementary information about the stricken ship. This may be interesting, but it has nothing to do directly with the main purpose of the news story, viz. to report the tragedy of a ship afire at sea.

So much for the reading of the news merely as a factual report of events. Let us now consider another type of writing found in the newspaper. It is what may be called interpretative or critical writing.

Critical Writing Interprets the News

A part of each newspaper is the straight reporting of events. Another aspect of each issue is the interpretations, the value judgments, and the journalistic appraisals of the significance of the day's happenings. In short, therefore, the modern journalist may be one of two types of writers: he may be a reporter and thus bring the news together for easy, comprehensive reading, presenting the facts and recounting the story of events as they happen. On the other hand, the modern journalist may be a critical interpreter of the news; and, as such, he fulfills a special role by showing the reader what, according to his broader understanding, the news means and what implications lie below the happenings and events of the day.

Each critical journalist usually writes within the area of his own special competence, as this has been enriched by years of experience or exceptionally intimate contact with some particular area of the day's news. Hence, such journalists write "special features" for the newspaper, such as an editorial, a syndicated column, the reviews of books, music, recordings, observations or comments on sports and sportsmen, and in a variety of similar areas for the purpose of giving to the readers of the paper a fuller understanding and insight into the meaning of the events which their fellow journalists report.

Thus, while the modern newspaper contains these two types of journalists and their writing, yet the role and functions of each must be clear and distinct. Each type of news writing must remain discrete and separate. It is likewise of greatest importance that there be no confusion in the mind of the reader as to the purposes of these two types of writing and that he recognize each the instant he comes upon one or the other in reading his daily paper.

Perhaps, before we look more intently at any examples of critical journalism, it might be well to ask what is the function of a critic. A critic, as we have suggested, is an interpreter for the masses of the meaning of events. In this sense the writer of editorials is a critic just as truly as the music or art critics or book reviewers. Nor is criticism, as is so often inferred, an essentially destructive approach: it is not basically faultfinding in the sense in which we so often employ the word in popular parlance. Criticism is, rather, the ability to see any event, whether it be local or world-wide in scope, in its proper perspective and framework in order to assess its meaning and significance.

To tell what has happened, that's news. To tell what the happening means in terms of its impact upon our everyday lives and the life of the nation and the world, that's criticism.

Critical writing demands certain skills and approaches on the part of the reader. Let us now consider how to read critical journalism. It may be well to begin by considering first how to read an editorial.

How to Read an Editorial

To read an editorial effectively, you must see clearly what the editorial writer is attempting to do. You must understand the way the editorial is structured and how the thought is developed.

Earlier in this book, under "How to Read the News," (pp. 93–94), we showed that from a structural standpoint a well-written news story is in effect an inverted pyramid with the broad informational base at the top; the rest of the pyramidal structure dwindles to details of lesser and lesser importance.

Generally, the writer of editorials reverses this structural pattern.

The editorial has one principal purpose: to set forth the position of the paper with respect to certain timely and important issues; and, if possible, to convert the reader to the writer's position, to convince the reader of the soundness of a particular editorial position.

The technique of the editorial is to present the evidence— the facts—first, and then to close in by means of a clinching sentence and to state unmistakably the editor's position. The punch line comes last. In general configuration, the editorial is also pyramidal but in conventional position: broad base down.

Let us take a typical editorial and analyze it. The editor of a college paper decides to do battle with the notion that college youth today are materially worse in behavior than formerly. He needs two things to convince the reader: the facts and a conclusion based squarely upon them. In order to illustrate clearly the technique of editorial writing, we shall, as in earlier instances, present the text of the editorial in the left-hand column with illustrative comments in the right-hand column.

ARE COLLEGE RIOTS SOMETHING NEW?

A recent essay in *Time* magazine points out that today's parents should take comfort in the recollection that, from the standpoint of the behavior of young people, things have certainly been worse. Riot and rebellion are a student tradition in the Western world. For example, in 1793 at Winchester, England, the high sheriff was summoned

An editorial is usually occasioned by some event or initiating incident; here, it is the comment in Time *magazine.*

Here is the main idea of the editorial, which the editor will hereafter bolster with factual examples.

after the students stoned the assistant headmaster with marbles. But the sheriff refused help because the students had firearms and were getting ready to defend themselves by flinging flagstones down on police. *Time* claims that at Harvard and Princeton the student episodes in this period were numerous. Professor Epiphalet Pearson kept what he called a Journal of Disorders. "In the hall at breakfast this morning," he noted, "bisket, tea cups, saucers, and a *knife* were thrown at tutors. At evening prayers the lights were all extinguished by powder and lead."

A list of college disturbances around the year 1815 includes one undergraduate dead in a duel at South Carolina College, several students shot at Ohio's Miami University, a professor killed at the University of Virginia, and the president of Mississippi's Oakland College stabbed to death by a student. Looking at the records of the time, duelling came also to Carlisle. A teacher visiting Jeremiah Atwater, then president of Dickinson, noted in respondence that, "The students are lawless as the whirlwind." In fact, two students engaged in a duel. A brief trustee record resolved, "That George

His first example comes from England, hence the appropriateness of the phrase "the Western world" rather than America.

Note reference to the Time *article again—the basis for this editorial. The scene now shifts to America: Harvard and Princeton. Note the word "numerous."*

In this paragraph the evidence piles up rapidly. Note the spread of violence over all the known United States of this period: Massachusetts (Harvard), New Jersey (Princeton), South Carolina, Ohio, Virginia, Mississippi, and (about to be mentioned) Pennsylvania.

The focus of attention narrows. Carlisle, Pennsylvania, is the site of Dickinson College. Now come the facts from the records of Dickinson College, for whose alumni this editorial was written.

Oldham be expelled and is hereby expelled from Dickinson College. . . . The trustees considered it but an act of justice to declare that his conduct in every other instance has been such as to meet their approbation and must express their regret that this sentence should be passed on a young man who had been so fair and conduct so exemplary."

History suggests that in our tendency to idealize youth we seem to forget what conditions were really like. It is safe to assume that compared with students of 150 years ago today's generation has come a long way. Or maybe the point is that while youth may be no worse today than in former time, college youth still have a long way to go.[2]

Now the editor begins editorializing. This paragraph is the broad base of the editorial. All of the facts that have already been presented rest upon these basic conclusions; and, after the facts have been presented, here is the attempt to convince the reader that college youth are certainly no worse today than formerly— but, he adds, maybe there is still room for improvement.

Editorials are, thus, simply expressions of opinion. They are written to provoke thought, to encourage discussion, to present a particular viewpoint for the reader's consideration. Hence, you should always remember that any editorial is the expression of but one man's viewpoint; and there are many ways of looking at any question.

Editorials are written to help you think constructively about the important issues of the day. You need not subscribe to their reasoning or, for that matter, agree with their conclusions; but, if you are to be intelligently well-read, you ought to give them at least serious attention.

[2] Adapted from *Dickinson Today,* Volume 3 (March, 1966), page 2.

Thus, the reader ought to ask certain questions with respect to the editorial which he has read:

1. Are the facts sufficient, and sufficiently to the point, to warrant the conclusions which the editorial writer draws from them?
2. Does the editorial writer state his position unmistakably at the conclusion of the editorial?

Since newspapers are usually classified in certain categories —conservative, liberal, or sensational—it might be well, for the sake of breadth of viewpoint, to read the editorial pages of two or more different types of newspaper. Lord Macaulay, you will recall, said that "men are never so likely to settle a question rightly as when they discuss it fully."

By the same token, it is equally true that men are never so likely to think clearly on any issue as when they consider it from different as well as differing points of view. And the places where these points of view are most readily accessible are in the editorial, the syndicated column, and the letters to the editor.

Technique for Reading the Editorial

How should you read the editorial so that you test it, in the reading of it, by the criteria given above? What is the way in which the effective reader attacks the editorial so that he gets the most from it for the amount of time he invests in reading it?

Here are some rules for reading not only the editorial but also related types of critical journalism. They are based upon the structure and the style of this genre of writing:

1. Read an editorial backward; begin with the last paragraph.
2. Next, go to the beginning and read downward through the editorial, noting the facts presented and how well they support the conclusion.
3. Finally, remember the editorial—like all Gaul—is divided

into three parts: the opening paragraphs which usually explain the *raison d'être* for the writing, the facts that support the conclusion, and the conclusion or editorial position. When reading an editorial, keep oriented.

Reading Other Critical Writing

Other critical writing might generally be handled in the same manner in which editorials are read. Book reviews, theater, music, and other reviews and critiques of artistic and creative efforts are essentially expressions of opinion. There are no canons of absolutism; the reviewer or the critic who regards a creative work usually approaches it impressionistically. The main question is, How does the work impress him; how does he feel about it? These questions ought never be answered in a narrow, selfish, or bigoted manner. It is the function of the critic to assist the reader, to guide him toward standards for judgment and bases for acceptance or rejection of a creative effort.

Each critic has certain standards he considers important and central to the evaluation of any artistic endeavor. We expect the critic to be intellectually alive and aesthetically sensitive. His review or critique should evidence these qualities. And not only this, but he should also evidence a competent knowledge of the art before him, considered and reviewed in a spirit of tolerance, magnanimity, and deep human understanding.

You might try reading the reviews and the critiques in the manner we have just outlined for the reading of editorials. Try reading all this type of writing backward: the conclusion first, then the rest of the review for the purpose of seeing the evidence, considering the supporting details, and weighing the merits of the judgments pro and con.

One leading New York publisher told me that each week he read *The New York Times Book Review* and the Herald-Tribune *Books,* cover to cover. "I read the last paragraph of each review," he said. "That is enough to give me the reviewer's opinion of the book. After all, that is what I want to know. If the conclusion is too startling, or if I am sufficiently aroused, I may glance over the rest of the review. But usually," he added, "the last paragraph or two is sufficient."

Reference has been made once or twice to the Letters-to-the-Editor column. In this department the readers of the newspaper express their own views and opinions with respect to matters that affect everyday life. Letters to the editor are usually alive, vital expressions of an aroused reader with respect to some happening or event which calls for spirited discussion and pointed comment. They are usually lively reading, and you should not overlook them as a piquant sauce in the diet of daily news reading.

And so, we have come to the end of the discussion of the two major types of writing which comprise the modern newspaper. We have looked at the newspaper from the standpoint of its value as a lifelong educative influence available to every adult. In this connection, you evaluated your own newspaper-reading habits in an attempt to assess your general interest and awareness of the stream of life as this stream courses through the columns of the daily press. We also looked at the techniques for surveying the contents and handling the newspaper most expeditiously, followed by suggestions on how to read the news, accompanied by a test for the appraisal of your own news-reading accuracy. Finally, the editorial and similiar types of critical journalism were discussed. There are, of course, other aspects of the daily paper, but we cannot here discuss these at length. Enough but to give one or two of them a passing glance.

Concerning the Funnies

The funnies are, however, worthy of passing attention since they command a towering readership among the American public. Eighty to a hundred million Americans read the comic

strips regularly in either the daily or the Sunday papers—
or both! This is almost twice as many as read the editorials.

The cartoon, which was the forerunner of the comic strip,
has had a long history. As early as thirty centuries B.C., the
Egyptians amused themselves and their contemporaries by
drawing and circulating cartoons of animals drawn on chips
of limestone and papyri.

Later, the Romans employed thin slabs of wood or slate
on which to draw their satiric cartoons and sold these in the
market place and in the Forum in the days of the Caesars.
In every crisis of the world's history, since ancient time, cartoons have helped to crystallize public feeling and to spur
decisive action. In the American Revolution, for example,
cartoons urged the colonists to "unite or die"; they lampooned
the king, lauded the goddess of liberty, and whipped up sen-
timent in behalf of the colonial cause. No less figures than
Benjamin Franklin and Paul Revere were the successful car-
toonists of those days. In France, Honoré Daumier ridiculed
Louis Philippe, depicting him in cartoons as Gargantua, and
sat in jail for his drawings. Both the Democratic donkey and
the Republican elephant first appeared as figments of cartoon-
ists' pens. Mention *Punch, Judge,* and *Mad* and at once we
are aware of magazines that have been given entirely to the
medium of the cartoon. Almost every home in America has
entertained at one time or another one or more of the following comic strip favorites as an intimate member of the family
—all are indigenous to American soil: the Yellow Kid, Jiggs
and Maggie, Foxy Grandpa, Mutt and Jeff, Krazy Kat, Little
Annie Rooney, L'il Abner, Starbuck, Felix, Popeye, the Kat-
zenjammer Kids, Donald Duck, Blondie, Pogo, Skeezix, Tar-
zan, Dick Tracy, and Batman.

Correspondingly, our language has been enriched with characteristic phrases of these comic strip characters, and our
standard repertoire of slang has been also enlarged: arf! arf!,
baloney, balls o' fire, crepe hanger, Dagwood sandwich, drug-

store cowboy, Dumb Dora, heebie jeebies, horse feathers, hot dog, hotsy totsy, sweet mama, the cat's pajamas,—to cite only a few of these.

Serious research and scholarly dissertations have also dealt with the comics. In 1962, Edward J. Robinson and David Manning White decided to find out, in a serious survey, "Who Reads the Funnies—and Why?"[3] They uncovered some startling and unexpected information:

1. Reading the funnies increases in direct ratio as education increases. College graduates by almost two to one read more comics than eighth graders. Graduate students and advanced-degree holders are the most avid of all comic strip readers.

2. Public opinion generally endorses the comics, and it regards them positively as a form of wholesome personal pleasure.

3. For children, the comics are a means of socializing with their schoolmates. Ninety-nine per cent of the boys and ninety-seven per cent of the girls surveyed indicated that they read one or more comic strips daily and that they preferred the humorous, non-narrative type of strip. Their response refutes the claim of certain critics of the comic strip that children principally seek elements of violence and sensationalism from comic strips.

4. Sunday comics readers peak at the age group from thirty to thirty-nine years, with a slow decline thereafter extending into the seventies.

5. Most Americans associate the comics with humor, happy times, and healthful, positive attitudes of mental and emotional stability.

The comics, then, are a great institution in the life of the average newspaper reader. They loom large in his inventory

[3] The complete report of this study may be found in "Comics Reading in America," Report No. 5, August, 1962; Communications Research Center, Boston University School of Public Relations and Communications, Boston, Massachusetts.

of items in the newspaper which he reads regularly. They have a philosophy and an outlook on life that is characteristically all their own. And the philosophy expressed in them is sometimes a deep, penetrating, and subtle commentary on the cartoonist's life and world view.

For those who would like more facts about the funnies— their history and their place in American life—a solid and readable book discusses their many-sided impact on our American culture. It is *The Funnies: An American Idiom,* edited by David Manning White and Robert H. Abel, and published by The Free Press of Glencoe, 1963.

For some of the facts appearing above, the author is generously indebted to this volume.

The Problem of Reading the Financial Page

As we have given a cursory glance to the comics, so this chapter would not be complete without an equally cursory glance at the problems which many readers experience in reading the financial sections of the newspaper. Although the comic strips have a readership that far outdistances that of the editorial, the financial pages of the newspaper are usually shunned by a great many readers—except for those who are particularly interested in investment or whose occupational demands are such that they must keep abreast of doings in the financial and business community.

Perhaps the least avid reader of the financial section is the American woman. And yet, this should not be so; for it is the financial section that influences perhaps more than any other department of the modern newspaper the life of the American woman and her family. For, it announces—frequently for the first time—the coming of new products; it keeps the housewife abreast of new developments that will affect not only her purse, but her home and her leisure time. The housewife may also find, in the column reporting department store sales and total retail business trends, some indication as to what the American woman will be wearing in the months ahead and what her family will be buying and using. The leading mail-order houses and chain-store systems also report their sales activity and their inventory turnover at stated intervals.

America is an industrial nation. Whatever affects the industry of the nation affects the nation's standard of living and the bank account of the individual American. Because of the importance of the national economy to every family, the financial pages of the leading news media report a broad, across-the-board picture of the economic health of the country. The weekly news magazines also usually carry at least a digest of the trends of business or some index to the state of the national prosperity. Because the modern journalist has tried to simplify the complexities of business, the reading of the financial section is, therefore, much less complex than generally thought and the business news is usually readily comprehensible to the average citizen.

Many readers have been scared away from the reading of the financial news because of its imagined involvement with associated areas that most Americans regard as deep, dark, and mysterious realms—economics, banking, exchange, and international trade. Most of this imagined horror is pure conjecture; for when you once begin to read the financial page, you will find that within a very brief time you are beginning to understand the business news and master the skill of reading this type of reporting.

At first you will be somewhat aware of and perhaps even a little disturbed by the specialized vocabulary which comes to the surface on any page dealing with business and finance. But you will soon learn to read the specialized terminology of business without any great trouble or difficulty. Here are some of the terms which may at first plague you: *ad valorem,*

Financial News to Be Sent by TV

General Telephone, Reuters to Start Service Jan 1.

By VARTANIG G. VARTAN

A financial news service combining the resources of Reuters, the leading British foreign news agency, and the General Telephone and Electronics Corporation will make its debut on Jan. 1, 1968.

The service will utilize a television display system similar to a home TV receiver. Receivers will carry the tapes of both the New York Stock Exchange and the American Stock Exchange, as well as the financial news report.

A "hard-copy" printout by teleprinter at a speed of 100 words a minute also will be available with the units. The coast-to-coast service envisages the brokerage community as its largest single market.

Michael E. Nelson, assistant general manager of Reuters, said the new service will be "fully competitive" with the financial news ticker of Dow Jones & Co., Inc. Dow Jones, estimated to have more than 4,000 news tickers in operation, also publishes The Wall Street Journal, Barron's and The National Observer, as well as a book enterprise.

The new service will be called the Reuter-Ultronic Report. Signals for the TV display will be transmitted over telephone circuits and Ultronic's own terminal equipment.

In June, the Ultronic Systems Corporation became a subsidiary of Sylvania Electric Products, Inc. Sylvania is a subsidiary of General Telephone. Ultronic was founded in 1960

COATS FOR FALL BEING REORDERED

Sportswear Is in Demand, Buying Offices Report

Stores continue to reorder fall coats, suits and sportswear, reports from resident buying offices indicate. Summaries for various departments follow:

WOMEN'S COATS AND SUITS: Activity centers on suede and leather coats, mink-trimmed coats and coat and suit outfits.

DRESSES: Sales of double wool knit outfits are excellent, as are sales of cocktail dresses, minidresses and daytime dresses.

SPORTSWEAR: A wide range of merchandise is in demand, including stretch slacks, sweaters, car coats, shells, tailored shirts and jumpers.

INTIMATE APPAREL: The strongest items include dusters, cotton dusters, nylon briefs, petticoats, pajamas and robe and gown sets. Baby dolls continue in demand.

WOMEN'S ACCESSORIES: Demand has intensified for watches with wide, novelty bands, pins, bracelets, earrings and necklaces, umbrellas and chain belts.

MEN'S CLOTHING AND FURNISHINGS: Sales of sweaters, raincoats, permanent-press slacks, sport shirts and car coats are active.

INFANTS' AND CHILDREN'S WEAR: Reorders are being written on playsuits, pajamas, toddler sets, raincoats and

Clerical-Job Salaries Up $4 a Week This Year

The average salary for 13 of the most representative clerical jobs in the United States is $91 a week, an increase of $4 over the 1966 average for the same job, the Administrative Management Society reports in its 1967 Survey of Office Salaries.

In Canada, the average weekly rate for these 13 jobs is $75, which also represents a $4 rise over the 1966 figure.

Data processing personnel also are earning more. The average rate in the United States for seven of the most representative positions in the field is $123 a week. As an example, the average weekly rate for intermediate systems analysts is $173. A top pre----

of 1966, while retailing in general is doing 4 to 5 per cent better. Chain store sales, as indicated by figures for a selected list of chain organization and catalogue houses, were up by 9.5 per cent in August and for the year to date by 6.9 per cent.

In the chain category of retailing, the variety and shoe stores are showing the best gains, but apparel and general merchandise stores are not very far behind. All of these stores are showing gains amounting to 10 to 15 per cent compared to the level of sales a year ago.

Significantly, the retail gains in soft goods lines are running well ahead of the rise in personal income. Third quarter personal income, according to figures in July and August will be 7 per cent larger than in the comparable quarter last year.

balance of trade, bank rate, bear market, gross national product, discount rate, gilt edged, ingot, stock split, and similar puzzlers. How many of them do you know?

If you are uncertain as to how well you know the meaning of these terms, why not turn to page 181? There you will find a test of your knowledge of business terms which occur frequently in the columns of the financial section of the paper. The test may serve two purposes: (1) to measure your own adequacy to understand the lingo of business and finance, and (2) to provide you with a beginning and elementary glossary of some terms to which you can add others as you discover them in the course of your reading.

For those who feel the need for some guidelines in understanding matters financial, some suggestions may be offered:

1. Make it a habit to read the business page regularly, even though you have not been reading it and you feel no interest at the moment in it.
2. Remember that current reporting practice in presenting financial news is not only to report the contemporary facts of business, but also to provide the reader with adequate background information and the rationale for understanding specific developments and trends.
3. Many of the larger financial and investment houses and the various federal reserve banks issue a monthly business news survey. Generally, you may secure these on written request. These discussions may help to give you a comprehensive survey of the financial scene; and, frequently, a regular reading of such news letters makes the financial page of the daily paper much more understandable.

Do you want a readable handbook which is slanted more in the direction of financial matters than those of business? Such a book is *How to Read the Financial News,* by C. Norman Stabler, now in its ninth edition, published by Harper and Brothers, New York.

In Conclusion

And so, when you drop your few pennies or your dime on the counter and pick up your daily paper, remember you have just purchased a document that has a word-count between 75,000 and 500,000 words—depending upon the size of the paper and whether it is a weekly or Sunday edition. That is the equivalent of from one to six fair-sized novels; and that is a lot of reading! Through the columns of your paper you look out upon the kaleidoscopic scene which represents the activities of modern man in an ever-changing world. Your paper brings you a first-hand account, through the eyes and the words of a host of reporters, of the happenings and events beyond the horizon, of numberless men and women whose thoughts, acts, and beliefs may alter tomorrow's headlines and change the course of history. The shadows of great men and little men, those of the famous and of the infamous, fall equally across the long corridors of newsprint.

Take up your paper with imagination; lay it down with deference, for you have been honored: you have been privileged to behold the world at a glance, and, under the aegis of a free press, to keep up with the relentless march of the day's news.

5. Reducing the pile
on the office desk

Rare is the man whose desk is not piled high!

For who of us is not behind the reading eight ball: reports to read, letters to digest, memos to note, and all the miscellaneous reading matter that clutters the office desk to be cleared away.

To make the pile vanish there is, unfortunately, no abracadabra, no magic formula, no fairy wand. Nor is there any trick of reading legerdemain which will free you from the daily burden of reading the important items carefully, attentively, and—at times—with utmost precision. Also true it is, and equally unfortunate, that this kind of reading takes time and demands effort and brain power, all of which puts a drain on those psychological factors which are so important in keeping up one's mental agility and reading efficiency.

But even with the assortment of reading tasks which are usually represented by the pile on the office desk and the demand these make on the latent psychological energy of the individual, you need not despair. You can attack that pile effectively and dispose of it forthrightly.

To this end, many of the hints that have already been given in this book are applicable in processing the reading of the workaday world and in getting it out of the way. But, in addition to the suggestions already given, there are specific ways of attacking the run-of-the-mill reading that comes with each morning's mail; and it is the purpose of this chapter to discuss some of these.

Reading Through the Eyes of the Man Behind the Desk

The man who sits behind today's office desk has perhaps a broader array of reading material presented to him in greater variety of written form and in far greater volume than any of his predecessors ever knew. He must handle typewritten letters and reports, handwritten memos, printed regulations, mimeographed announcements, and, in addition, he must constantly do battle with flimsy onionskin and the fuzzy letter shapes of countless carbon copies. Add to this the mélange of reading fare of one or two newspapers—the *Wall Street Journal, The New York Times,* or the local press—printed in small type on pulp stock; one or more magazines: the periodicals, trade journals, and professional publications that business and professional men must read regularly if they are to escape the accusation of "not keeping up" with the march of events and recent advances in their own vocations and professions; and you have some idea of the widely disparate reading tasks with which the man behind the desk must contend each day.

Reading these various kinds of material requires constant change of pace and constant accommodation to new styles, types, and varieties of writing, which, in turn, increases fatigue and lays a heavy demand on the daily store of energy of the individual reader.

By taking a hint from what we have just said, let us attack the problem of reducing the pile on the office desk by keeping together all the items of a particular type of reading. By so doing you can save time, conserve energy, and make haste against the adverse conditions inherent in business reading generally.

Fortunately, business readers are adaptable. They soon learn to accept a particular type of writing and to tolerate certain impeding factors so long as they can maintain, for a sustained period, consistency in the same type of reading. Furthermore, they become more efficient as they become acclimated to the particular reading milieu into which they have been cast. This, then, brings us to the first rule for attacking the pile on the office desk.

Don't read until you sort

Efficiency begins the moment you face the pile. Watch the fellow who does not know how to attack that pile, and what he does will be thoroughly revealing as to how important the right start is. The uninitiated one will dip in, opening, unfolding, reading whatever his fingers touch first. Result: he opens a letter and reads it, then he unfolds a memo, followed by a printed announcement, and so on, constantly reorganizing and reorienting himself and his reading focus to every new format, presentation, and situation. He evidences the marks of one who does not know how to cope with the job on the desk before him.

Rather than attack the pile willy-nilly, and without plan or forethought, dip in and take a handful of the reading material to which you must give attention. Don't begin to read until you sort. Place on separate piles the same type of reading material: memos on one pile, newspapers on another, professional journals and printed materials on still another. Sort out the letters. Put these together. This will assist in getting most of the typewritten matter in one pile. There is a purpose for this, for typewritten material presents problems of its own.

You should be aware of the fact that typewriter face, in contrast to type face, is comparatively difficult to read. The characters of the typewriter have none of the subtle gradations of light and heavy strokes, no shift of mass or heft of balance. Each typewritten character has the same typographical characteristics: flat, thin, lifeless.

Remember also that visibility is reduced when reading the typewritten page. Try an experiment. Take a magnifying glass—even a low-powered one will illustrate the point—and look at the characters on this page of your book. What do you see? The printed page has razor-sharp, jet-black characters on a white, nongloss page. Each letter has gentle gradations of thick and thin strokes which seem to give the letter stability, balance, symmetry. A line of such letters is restful and easy to read.

Now pick up a typewritten letter, preferably a letter *not* written on an electric typewriter, and inspect the typewritten characters with a magnifier, the same as you did for printed type. What do you see this time? If it is run-of-the-mill typing, you will see a fuzzy, gray, ragged imprint of each letter, the contour of which is made up of minute dots from the weave of the typewriter ribbon. Electric typewriters are somewhat better with respect to visibility, but even these are mostly thin and, in addition, some electrics have a sans-serif type which militates against fleetness of the eye across the line.

Research has shown that typewriter face is considerably more arduous to read than is conventional print. Typewritten material puts a 5 per cent drag-loss on the speed of the average reader. When materials are mimeographed or spirit duplicated, the drag-loss and impedance of speed is even more, perhaps as much as 6 to 8 per cent.

There is nothing, of course, that you can do to improve your visual road conditions. You will have to travel at a reduced rate of speed in all probability, and it may be well for you to recognize and to accept the fact. But you can compensate somewhat for less than optimal reading conditions, for you can structure the reading situation so that you can make haste skillfully. Put all the same type of reading material together, from a typographical standpoint, and you have so arranged your reading task that you can the better adapt your skill to the stretch of reading before you and, hence, gain in acclimatization what you might otherwise lose in shifting from one type of readability to another.

Study the unique style and characteristics of each type of writing

Think of each of the piles which you have just created as containing a discrete and a particular-skill-centered type of writing. A specialized set of skills will be needed, therefore, for the reading of the material in each pile. You do not read letters, for example, as you read newspapers. Newspapers we have already considered; and you are quite aware, for example, that the style and structure of the news story is quite different from that of the editorial. The knowledgeable reader, however, handles each with the same deftness and ease because he knows what to look for and how to get the most meaning in the least amount of time. And for the reading of the pile that contains the *Wall Street Journal* and *The New York Times*, the application of these skills is indispensable. Letters, likewise, have their own distinctive structure and mode of expressing the thought. By appreciating some of the general characteristics and the typical thought structure of the several various kinds of writing which cross the business-man's desk, we can the better know what to look for and where to find it—quickly, concisely, and with the least loss of motion.

Reading the Business Letter

Since, perhaps, the bulk of the reading matter that comes

across the desk of the average businessman is in the form of letters and general correspondence, it may be well to look first at this type of reading task.

A business letter can usually be divided into three parts:

1. The gracious, but largely meaningless beginning;
2. The burden of the message; and
3. The quiet afterglow and the graceful bowing out.

Let us discuss each of these parts in somewhat more detail. Consider the average letter. It usually begins: "In reply to your inquiry of . . . ." Of course, it is! You wrote the A.B.C. Corporation two weeks ago, didn't you, to inquire of them about a particular matter? The very sight of their envelope on your desk reminds you that the letter is probably "in reply to your inquiry."

But while our principal aim is to be as straightforwardly efficient as possible, let us not be discourteous or rude in any remarks or assertions which we may utter with respect to opening paragraphs.

The opening paragraph is a graceful way of initiating communication. It has its proper place, just as a genial handshake and a few words of greeting have their rightful place at the beginning of a business conference. Before you sit down to do business, you begin with the conventional pleasantries and appropriate protocol. The *pièce de résistance*—the discussion of the matter for which the conference was held—is yet to come. Have an eye open for the gracious amenities at the beginning of a letter, accept them in the spirit in which they were meant, but if you are in a hurry, get down to business and go straight to the heart of the message.

Usually a letter will consist of three or four paragraphs. If that is so, then shoot for mid-page. Here is where the heart of the matter is likely to be found. When you strike paragraph two, your alertness should go up. Enter it alertly and with expectation. This may be just more warm up, or it may be the principal thing the writer of the letter wishes to convey to you. After a very few words you will, however, recognize the nature and the tenor of the thought.

Letter reading demands rapid change of pace. Some parts of the letter, so far as the purpose for which the letter is written, are largely inconsequential and may be dispatched with no more than a glance. But where the principal message appears, you will want to proceed with care and attention. That place is usually in the vicinity of mid-page. There the writer will state his principal argument, propose a matter for consideration, or concentrate all his logic and reasoning to convince you that you should weigh carefully and adopt the course of action which he is proposing. Here, then, is the place where, on the basis of the letter, you may have to make a decision; where you may have to reply to a proposition which the writer has laid before you; or where you may have to take action in the light of the message which the letter contains.

Usually, letters end as they begin, with a few amenities and a terminal flourish. The writer expresses the hope, for example, that he will hear from you favorably; he hopes to hear from you soon; he wishes you good luck and the best of health. It is thoughtful; it is courteous; and, psychologically, it is astute and always good business to leave you in a resolved and happy frame of mind. Furthermore, it shows that the writer knows the social proprieties.

You may note the gentility of the writer, but should you be running behind schedule and the pressure be on you to reduce the pile on the office desk, you may at this point depress your reading acceleration pedal and speed out of the letter as, in motoring, you speed out of a little hamlet, noting its charm the while but pressing to be on your way.

A simple procedure, then, for attacking most business letters may be spelled out as follows:

The first act in reading a business letter is to sweep down over the entire letter with a single glance. Your purpose in doing so is to note the length of the letter, to judge its paragraphing, and to estimate as nearly as possible by inspection where the principal message of the letter may perhaps lie. See as much as you possibly can with that first lightning glance.

Next, go back to the beginning of the letter; let your eye drop down the left-hand margin. Read the opening words of each paragraph.

Paragraph one begins, for example: "We appreciate your letter . . ." Good, you say to yourself, I'm glad they do, but—. And so, spend no more time on this paragraph but get on to the next.

Paragraph two begins: "We are enclosing the material . . ." This you already know. The material tumbled out of the envelope when you opened it. No need to read further. But, give this paragraph a further passing glance, and get on.

Paragraph three: "We offer you substantial discounts in our product which will make your interest in it very worthwhile." Whoa! Let's take it easy. Now here we're talking business! Let's see what the proposition is. Read the paragraph carefully and comprehendingly.

Paragraph four: "Thank you for giving this letter your attention . . ." Ah, the gentle end and a graceful bowing out. Like the beginning, it is thoughtful and considerate, and it closes the letter on a note that makes you feel that if these people are this thoughtful perhaps you might want to consider their proposition a little further. Though it is not strictly an essential part of the statement of proposition, yet this paragraph does have its function in wrapping up the matter tactfully and deferentially.

Finally, note well the signature. Here is the name of the individual making you the offer. A speaker is always important, especially if he says anything that merits your attention or, even more, that affects your pocketbook.

And so, on to the next letter in the pile.

One final word, however, with respect to the reading of business letters. Remember that these are workaday messages written by people who are essentially very much like yourself. Many who write them disclaim, in fact, any proficiency with the written word and frankly confess their own inadequacy in putting thought to paper. You must be prepared, therefore, to encounter some shortcomings of those who generally write acceptably but not professionally. The average man is not always as sensitive to the precise word, the exact phrase, the grammatical nuance of structure, and the rhetorical matters of unity and coherence as the professional writer is.

The very fact that most letters are written, or dictated, by overburdened men in workaday jobs may have several implications so far as the skill of reading business letters is concerned.

First, when reading the business letter, let us not take too literally the paragraph as a pure structural unit of writing. A carefully constructed paragraph is a work of art. It is the product of consummate compositional skill, the result of unity of thought and coherence of utterance. Not all of us have the facility of expression nor the talent with language that is necessary to write structurally sound and rhetorically excellent paragraphs. In consequence, many business letter paragraphs will be inchoate, structurally defective; and, as a result, they cannot be read strictly in accordance with the guidelines for the reading of a paragraph which were proposed in the earlier part of this book.

Reading a business letter, therefore, is a cooperative effort between writer and reader. You, as reader, should be prepared to meet the writer of the letter halfway and to assist him in communication where he may have failed to be entirely precise or perfectly articulate. Bring your best thought and all your reading skills to the reading of the business letter. By so doing you will help the author and—what is even more important—you will help yourself to get the thought clearly, concisely, and quickly.

One further matter should be mentioned. Beware of the cliché; translate the trite phrase. In writing business letters it is easy to rely upon the worn phrase, the hackneyed expression, and the stock jargon of the trade.

Really read, with mind alert and sensitive for meaning, and business jargon will frequently become a threadbare collection of phrases that convey little thought in the noisy clatter of syllables that clutter the page.

Take, for example, "We regret to inform you that your order cannot be filled at this time." That is so much nonsense. Read with any awareness at all and you will see through the sham and pretense. The writer does not really regret. To regret means, literally, "to mourn for the dead" (If he means what he says and really *does* "regret," what does that make you?); it means "to weep" or "feel remorse." Certainly, he does not "regret" that he must "inform" you. The truth is, he probably couldn't care less, and to write to you is just one of his workaday chores. Why not say, "We cannot fill your order now." To have written thus would have been ever so much more truthful, forthright, and verbally economical. A mere six words replace a noisy, bombastic fourteen. In 57 per cent fewer words, the streamlined version eliminates the noise and fustian of useless words.

Read the average business letter and you will recognize how commonplace these pompous, low-efficiency phrases are: "We feel certain that you will find . . . ," the letter begins. Then it pleads, "Please be assured that we are investigating the matter . . ." and "as soon as we have completed our investigation, we shall communicate with you . . ."—all of which adds up to exactly: "We shall find out and write you."

Therefore, in reading the jargon of business you may often need to gather up whole armloads of words and to compress them into one succinct phrase by telling yourself, "All that the man is *really* saying is. . . ." This helps comprehension, aids speed, and helps to clear away the verbal smog. As a reader, you are also meeting the writer halfway by clarifying for him what he is probably incapable of clarifying in his own writing.

Reading the Trade Papers and Professional Journals

Every businessman's desk gathers its share of periodicals, journals, trade papers, newsletters, and similar printed items. Unlike typewritten letters, these periodical items are usually easy to read because most of them are set in printer's type and their contents are prepared by professional writers. Thus, they have more organization and form and may have some of the most objectionable jargon deleted.

Some suggestions for handling this type of material are:

1. *Dive for the index.* Many journals and periodicals list the contents of the issue in an index which is printed, often, in Reader's Digest fashion, on the front cover of the periodical; or else it appears a page or two under the front cover. Here is the key to the periodical, the master guide to its contents. As soon as you pick up the periodical, beeline your way to the index.

2. *Keep a note pad handy.* Use it to jot down the page references of the articles which interest you and to which you will want to refer. By so doing you will not need to waste time, once you have begun to read, thumbing back through the journal to find the index again and, having found it, to hunt your way again through the jungle of titles to locate the next one you would like to read.

3. *Grasp the outline at a glance.* Because most periodical

articles are professionally written and edited, they contain a structuralized outline in the form of subheadings throughout the article. The mark of a tyro reader is that he begins reading without a preliminary exploratory survey. Having flipped to the article, take in its organization by skimming it. Thumb through it. Employ the techniques we suggested on pages 77–85. Read only the first sentence of each paragraph. That may be all you need. On the other hand, if there are interesting sections or important passages in it, these may merit your full attention.

4. *Search for a summary.* Look for a prepared summary of the contents. Technical articles usually contain these. They are located usually either up front or just before the bibliography at the end of the article. If there is such a summary, read it first. It will give you the ground plan of the article, and an outline against which you may read in more detail if this seems, upon further inspection, to be advisable.

5. *Arm yourself with a red pencil.* If the journal is expendable, and does not circulate to other readers, have a red pencil handy. Mark the important paragraphs. If there are no subheadings and, in reading, you discern the outline and organization of the article, be your own editor. Jot down in the margin the appropriate subheadings. A few words will suffice, but let them collectively comprise an outline of the thought.

6. *Clip it.* As for trade papers, newsletters, and similar ephemeral materials, you may be interested in only one or two items in the whole issue—or in nothing at all. Keep a pair of scissors near you in addition to your red pencil. If what you see interests you, clip it. You may relegate the rest of the document to the wastebasket. To learn to throw out judiciously is one of the prime secrets in reducing the pile on the office desk.

6. Reading with your eyes wide open

Print has a way of hypnotizing you.

Depending upon the skill with which the words are set down, you—like many a reader—may be lulled by the magic of the words themselves into acting as though the word were indeed the fact; and by responding, consequently, in accordance with the way in which the author would have you react, you may quite unsuspectingly fall into the verbal snare which he has set for you.

The aim of most writing is to influence the reader. Every writer, in fact, writes with one eye on his manuscript and the other eye on you, his reader. He never lets you get out of his sight, nor does he ever forget that you are a human being with sensitive reactions upon which he can play in one way or another. He writes as he does because he hopes to influence you to conform to his desires, to adopt his viewpoint, to think his thoughts. All promotional literature, all advertising has but one aim—reader reaction. The persuasive magic of the printed word is the secret weapon of the propagandist.

Read with critical discrimination, and you will approach the page with your eyes wide open. You will recognize at once the spell which the printed word casts upon you. When you read with your eyes wide open, you read also with your mind fully alive and vitally alert. To read in this manner is to read critically.

Critical reading is a battle of wits. it is, on the one hand, the persuasiveness of the writer and his skill in enlisting the dynamic power of words to convince the reader that he should obey the writer's suggestions. On the other hand, it is a keen and sensitive recognition of the writer's artfulness that immunizes the reader against the infectious nuances of meaning so that the persuasiveness of the author's words and their motivational effect should not catch the reader off guard, thus forcing him to acquiesce blindly where he should meet the words with his eyes wide open and his mind fully aware of the designs and purposes of the writer.

So, then, both writer and reader are active participants in critical reading. They are contenders in a logomachy—a tussle of words—with one of them on the offensive, the other on the defensive. Each is engaged to outflank the other in a wordy battle of wits. Even if you adopt the words of the writer as a basis for action, you should do so knowingly and of your own free choice.

Guidelines for Critical Reading

If, then, you are to read critically, there should be some ground rules, some basic approaches to the page which should make the critical reading of that page more systematic and more intelligent. What are these?

Reading so that you are fully aware of the author's thought and purpose requires that you be cognizant of such fundamental guidelines for accurate and effective critical reading.

1. *Know precisely what the words say.* Many people read by impression. They "think" they know what the words mean. They have a "general idea" what the author is saying. Ask them to translate into their own words, in clear, succinct equivalent language, the thought which the words on the page

express, and they will look at you, lost and bewildered. Such "reading" is not reading. Actually, it is only fuzzy and obscure impressionism which nets the reader precisely nothing.

It is amazing how many readers do not really know what the words say, what the thought is, or what message the writer has for them. They are hypnotized by verbiage. In such an atmosphere of fog and obscurantism, critical reading is impossible.

The touchstone, therefore, which will determine whether you are prepared to read critically is always the question: Exactly what do the words say? What do they mean, literally?

Take, for example, this statement on the carton of Sparkle Fang toothpaste:

> Sparkle Fang has been shown to be an effective decay-preventive dentifrice that can be of value when used in a conscientiously applied program of oral hygiene and regular professional care.

Good! A product which has a statement like that on the carton *must* be wonderful! It sounds so professional—so convincing! And, furthermore, it's not merely a statement; it's a *quotation*. These are the words of the Committee on Therapeutics of the American Dental Association. That makes it authentic.

The above is the way the normal person reads or, rather, reasons. Let's look at the statement now for the sole purpose of discovering exactly what these words mean. We shall consider it phrase by phrase; and perhaps in trying to clarify some of the more obscure points, we shall ask some very simple—almost naive—questions as we proceed. But, remember, our sole purpose is merely to find out *precisely* what the statement is saying.

The statement begins: Sparkle Fang "has been shown to be an effective decay-preventive dentifrice." It "has been shown"

—to whom? Who specifically observed this decay-preventive quality of Sparkle Fang? And on what type of teeth? Conceivably, it could have been tested for its "decay-preventive" quality on *dentures!* It says nothing—nor even implies anything—to the contrary. And what does "effective" mean? Where is the line of demarcation where the effectiveness of a dentifrice stops and ineffectiveness begins?

By this time you probably sense that a careful, critical reading of this statement leaves the reader somewhat in open-ended bewilderment.

But the statement goes on: ". . . that can be of value . . . ." Notice the verb. It does not say that it *will* be of value. That's a guarantee! Rather, it states merely that it has the possibility of being of value. Which means exactly what? And what is "value"?

The fog thickens. Let's turn to another phrase.

". . . when used in a conscientiously applied program . . . ." When used . . . in a program! How does one *use* a dentifrice *in a program?* Dentifrices are usually *used* for brushing the teeth, but here it plainly says that Sparkle Fang "can be of value when used in a . . . program." Could it conceivably be that this is the only time it can be of value—when used in a program and not on the teeth?

But there's a further consideration, for he who reads critically would like to have answered at this point another question: What has conscience—the ability to tell moral right from wrong in behavior and to determine ethical standards of goodness—to do with Sparkle Fang and the fact that it can be of value? Yet the statement says quite plainly that Sparkle Fang is a dentifrice "that can be of value when used in a *conscientiously* applied program." How do you apply a program conscientiously? Applied? What does that mean? How applied? Applied to what? Certainly you must apply something *to* something. When I purchased Sparkle Fang I assumed that sooner or later Sparkle Fang would be applied to the teeth, but here—if I read correctly—I am told that "the program" is to be applied!

Now I am groping in fog!

". . . a conscientiously applied program of oral hygiene and regular professional care." What is a *program* of oral hygiene? Does that mean brushing the teeth with Sparkle Fang only? Should one add an antiseptic mouth wash to the ritual? Employ a germicidal or antibiotic spray? One? Two? All three? If so—and whatever it means—how often should this ritual of "oral hygiene" be practiced so that it may be a "conscientiously applied program"?

Come to think of it, what is "regular professional care"? How often is regular? Once a month? Once a year? Twice a year? And what is "professional care"? My physician is a professional man, also my attorney, and my clergyman. They all "care" for me in one way or another: physically, legally, or spiritually. Any of these may afford me "professional care." Of course, since the statement appears on a dentifrice carton, I *assume* by sheer association that what is meant is professional *dental* care, but in a court of law I would have to swear that nothing that I read says so, nor even implies as much. Am I supposed to guess? Nothing that I read tells me that either. At this point, I am completely bewildered.

What *does* the statement quoted above mean? Who knows? Is there any way to find out?

Since all our efforts so far seem to have gone for naught, let's try another approach. Perhaps we can reconstruct the message if we suggest some ideas. Does the statement simply say: Use Sparkle Fang four times each day, go to your dentist twice a year for an examination, and you'll have less tooth decay? No, it emphatically does *not* say that. Millions of Americans, however, who pick up the carton and, on the basis of the statement, purchase Sparkle Fang *think* that is what it says—or something similar.

Read the statement critically, and you will find, in fact, that it says very little, though it makes much fuss in creating an incomprehensible verbal noise and gives an impression that it *is* saying something very important.

This is gobbledygook and verbal obfuscation at its worst. And it is not rare to encounter it in everyday reading. Some so-called professional "literature" in every profession belongs to this type of writing. Gobbledygook, jargon, and profession-alese make much noise to utter very little. To shrivel and disintegrate it to its true size, subject it to the scrutiny of a few searching questions. Critical reading is learning to read acutely and is aided by developing the skill of learning to ask a few searching questions.

And so, the first rule for critical reading is: *Read interrogatively; ask questions of the text to discover what it really is saying—precisely.*

Beware of the Appeal!

Most writers are excellent practical psychologists. They write as they do because your mind works as it does. Consequently, they choose their words with infinite care. Choosing the word, the writer then sets it in his writing with meticulous discrimination; for he seeks a precise, yet unobtrusively subtle, impact of each word on the mind of the reader just as an artist mixes his pigments with delicate care because of the total effect that the artist wishes to create in the eye of the beholder. Since it is, however, in the mind of the reader that the author seeks his ultimate result, he so chooses and places his words that their combined impact will result in a carefully levelled and well-aimed appeal to the reader's emotional as well as his intellectual responses.

Here, then, is where you, as reader, need to know the appeal techniques and psychological booby traps of the author. For, when you have been cued in on his appeal battery, you then can assess more accurately what he says and evaluate more intelligently his reason for saying it. In short, you will read his words with increased comprehension and greater understanding.

What are these appeals? Generally speaking, they are seven:

1. The appeal to the reader's pocketbook
2. The appeal to the reader's egotism
3. The appeal to the reader's curiosity
4. The appeal to share with others
5. The appeal to the supernatural, the mysterious, the unusual
6. The appeal to the reader's sense of beauty
7. The appeal to the reader's sense of spiritual and moral values.

The torrent of print that rolls from the presses daily overwhelms most readers and subjects them to these psychological forces and emotional appeals without their being aware of what is happening. And it is a bewildering experience to be caught in such a deluge without being competent to assess its effect or to identify the seven tributaries above that make up its power and channel their energy into better reading and greater awareness. Let us, therefore, analyze these appeals in more detail.

The appeal to the reader's pocketbook. Is it the speech of a spellbinding politician urging cuts in government spending, or a do-it-yourself manual that bids you save cash by being your own craftsman and handy man? Or perhaps it is the yellow section of the telephone book or an advertisement in the daily paper that tells you where you can buy at savings and to best advantage. Conceivably, it is a bank which invites you by way of the printed word to place your earnings in its trust so that your earnings will earn still more. In all of these instances, the sole purpose of the writing is to address your pocketbook and to talk to you in terms of dollars and cents. We could multiply the examples *ad infinitum.* Increase your awareness at this point and note how much contemporary print speaks to you in terms of the pocketbook.

The appeal to the reader's egotism. Does the writing address you as a person of importance? Perhaps it tells you that you can study at home and make your mark as a well-trained and successful technician. It promises you that your sagacity in choosing a particular brand name will make you "a man of distinction." If you are a housewife, it assures you that by using X-brand detergent you can have "the whitest wash in town" and, by implication, be the envy of the whole community.

The writing addresses itself to your egotism; it flatters your personal esteem. Generally, you feel better for having read the words. It has accomplished what the author of the words set out to do: given you a psychological and emotional lift. He has scored a direct hit.

The appeal to the reader's curiosity. Man is the most curious of animals. He eternally wants to know. All education is directed to this one end: the satisfaction of intellectual curiosity. Quiz games and playing Trivia find their popularity because of this characteristic of human nature. Look over any paperback stand and note the number of titles which represent purely informational books: *A Pictorial History of Western Art, The Listener's World of Classical Music, Mathematics for Everyone, A Parent's Guide to Child Development,* and on and on you may go—titles which draw from every area of man's knowledge, from economics to astrophysics, from history to the world of tomorrow. They have all been written with one aim in the mind of their authors: to satisfy man's insatiable curiosity.

The appeal to share with others. Man is not only innately curious, he is incurably gregarious. He likes to live in company with other humans; and, in so doing, he likes, furthermore, to share with them his experiences which he has found interesting or rewarding. For this reason newspapers flourish. What goes on around the world as well as what happens in the local village provides news reading for millions. A bomb explodes, a politician harangues a crowd, the town council enacts an ordinance, Congress passes a law, the Supreme Court hands down a decision, a personal mishap befalls a neighbor, the bells of the church ring for a wedding or toll for a funeral, a citizen of the community is awarded recognition for meritorious service, a school has a festival, a club holds a cook-out —all these events provide opportunity for us to share with others what we ourselves have found important and worthwhile. Newsmen and journalists know this. These are the events that keep the news presses of the world rolling.

Combine man's insatiable curiosity with his desire to live with others and to share with them his good fortune and his bad, and you have some explanation for the news media of the world.

As a critical reader, you pick up your morning paper; and in so doing you, figuratively, push back the curtain upon a stage where men and women have their exits and their entrances; and each one in his time plays many parts. You stand aloof, but you look down upon a world where human beings living together provide the drama of each day's events. And, as a critical reader, you regard those events cinematographically: as little frames of human activity which, taken together, provide a meaningful commentary on the life of the world around you and the day in which you live.

The appeal to the supernatural, the mysterious, and the unusual. Man has always been fascinated by what he has not understood. The mysterious, the supernatural, the bizarre, the unusual has ever intrigued him. The unremitting search for what is beyond the substance of this world accounts for the fascination of mankind with mythology and fairy tales. It also accounts for the perennial popularity of the "whodunit," the deluge of mystery novels and tales, the interest in accounts of unidentified flying objects, and even the preoccupation with death. These all are manifestations of man's eternal fascination with and interest in the supernatural and the unfathomable.

Authors know this proclivity in man, and so they write mystery novels and incredible tales of the unknown. Advertisers know it; and as a result, they appeal to the power of the mysterious to fulfill their extravagant claims.

Notice how many times words suggesting the miraculous, the supernatural, the magical confront you on all sides from advertising blurbs and sales slogans. "Tastes like a mint; works like a *miracle!*" "*Fantastic* window spray leaves your windows *inconceivably* clean!" "Let *magic* eye be the mighty *giant* to guard your home while you are away!" "As *indescribably* comfortable as sleeping on a moonbeam!" (That would be an unusual and supernatural feat indeed!) "Buy powerful new Kleen with the *miraculous* whitener which will leave your clothes *fantastically* fresh and *exotically* soft."

Those slogans are loaded with otherworldliness. When a writer appeals to what is unbelievable, to what is fantastic, to what is magical and miraculous, to what is bizarre and inconceivable, he is also appealing to an aspect of human nature which still likes to believe in stories of the imagination and the never-never-land of Jonathan Swift, Lewis Carroll, and Walt Disney. And there is a lot of writing and a lot of appeal of that kind.

The appeal to the reader's sense of beauty. The latest model of a popular car was on the showroom floor. The salesman had just handed to the prospective buyer a descriptive booklet detailing the allure of the mechanical beauty:

> The Skid Wagon is solid, silent, and elegant. The invitingly clean interior with rich warm color gives you a dazzling introduction to power. That power is seen in the devastatingly beautiful low sweep of line and stunning contour that makes the magnificent Skid Wagon the most luxurious, trim, and handsome car on the road today.

The appeal to the buyer is of the beauty of the machine. Note the terms that bespeak that beauty: "solid, silent, and elegant," "the invitingly clean interior," "rich warm color," "a dazzling introduction to power," "the devastatingly beautiful low sweep of line and stunning contour," "magnificent," "the most luxurious, trim, and handsome car on the road."

Most readers fail to recognize the recurrent insistence of the author. But, it is usually there, and the wise reader has his eye open for it. Here, that insistence is on beauty. It is there—unmistakably. Out of fifty-four words, thirty-seven directly address themselves to the reader in terms of the beauty of the car. That is almost 70 per cent of the total wordage.

Nor is this accent on beauty unusual in our modern world. Pick up almost any magazine and the emphasis it places on the beautiful is a major part of its appeal. From cover girl to the last illustration, the pictorial emphasis is on loveliness and beauty: houses and cars, hair and complexion, fabrics and food—all come in for their part in the spotlight. And words reinforce the pictures. Open the magazine and read a paragraph or two. You will be impressed by the graphic speech and picturesque language.

Nowadays, most writing is vibrant, alive, vital. It cannot be inert or colorless and have a readership of the mass of modern Americans. For that reason, writers are sensitive people. They mold their thought with words, delicate or bold, as the occasion demands. They employ figures of speech so that their thought may be cast in stronger line with greater power of appeal.

For many years, the *Reader's Digest* has conducted a regular feature under the heading, "Toward a More Picturesque Speech." In this feature the reader is made aware of the brilliance and wit of words. For example, winter may be merely the slush and slop of city streets, or it can be the magnificence of "wailing winds and naked woods, and meadows brown and sere"; a season in which the leafless trees become "bare, ruined choirs, where late the sweet birds sang"; and where "the frolic architecture of the snow" mimics "slow structures, stone by stone."

The Sunday edition of *The New York Times* has for many years concluded its editorial columns with a brief paean of praise in celebration of some timely happening or in joyous exaltation of some season of the year or aspect of nature. Like the glowing color of a sunset, the outstanding characteristic of this final editorial is its beauty—its charm of thought, its grace of expression. It illustrates how the English language may be employed in the hands of a sensitive and experienced writer. Here, for example, is one of these editorials, entitled "Autumn Cargoes." It was an October editorial in the Sunday *Times* several years ago.[1]

Read it with a feeling for the delicacy and the power of its expression, for nuance of sound, for shade and color of word and phrase, for shadowy suggestion and brilliant insight. Read it thus and you read it critically; and instead of just so much newsprint, the following editorial becomes a bright linguistic pageant of sound and color and rhythmic motion.

[1] *The New York Times*, Sunday, October 7, 1962, section E, page 8.

Autumn Cargoes

Brooks and rivers now are laden with the autumn harvest. The watery currents carry a vast armada of leafy colors, a sampling from every bankside tree upstream, and their eddies are like the swirling strokes of a whimsical artist playing with exotic pigments. Watch a stream for ten minutes and you will have seen autumn flowing past, as leisurely as time itself.

But if you would see the dazzle and variety of this seasonal cargo, watch the airy rivers, the winds. See how a breeze invites a milkweed pod to dispatch its silken freight to far places, how it shimmers and dances as the floss spills forth. See the way a wind curls across a meadow, pausing an instant at each thistle head, how it shines with frothy fluff as it goes on. See how a wind in a bogland tests the brown thumbs of the cattails, how it becomes a current of misty silk as the ripe heads release their shimmering ripeness, light as fog.

The wind has its common cargo too, the leaves themselves, and it discusses this phase of business in crisp terms in every gutter and at every roadside. And it even has its live passengers. A midmorning breeze will pluck a dozen spiderlings from a weed patch, each tiny spider riding a self-made silken strand. A north wind will sometimes be briefly orange with a flight of monarch butterflies on their way south.

It is a varied cargo, this autumn freight, and it rides every stream that flows on or over the earth.

Having read that, you must feel as though you have heard an autumnal fantasia from the throat of a mighty organ with all its pipes, great and small, speaking in a vast array of mood and motif. At least, think of it as such for a moment.

The editorial begins with a colorful movement, stating the theme: the "watery currents" of brooks and rivers laden with "a vast armada of leafy color" are swirling, eddying, like "a whimsical artist playing with exotic pigments." The movement is broad, slow, adagio—autumn majestically flowing past "as leisurely as time itself."

Then the mood changes, the tempo quickens, and the airy flutes speak of the dazzle and variety of the seasonal cargo, this time borne not on the bosom of the slow waters of the earth, but on the agile and graceful rivers of the wind. Personification subtly lends charm to language.

Behold "a breeze *inviting* a milkweed pod to dispatch its silken freight." See that same breeze cavorting in bogland, testing the "brown *thumbs* of the cattails" to see if it can disintegrate them into "a current of misty silk, light as fog."

A bassoon-like subtheme of the fantasia develops. The wind and the leaves discuss "business" "in crisp terms in every gutter and at every roadside."

Now, the movement grows more animated. Live passengers join the stream of denizens that the wind bears aloft: spiderlings on silken strands and an orange cloud of monarch butterflies.

Finally, we reach the last paragraph and the brief finale of the fantasia of autumn. The opening theme returns, this time including all the currents in both earth and sky. You are left with the vision of the "varied cargo, this autumn freight" gliding past on every stream of water or of wind that flows either "on or over the earth."

How about it? Were you aware of this complex of thought, this intricate working out of mood and theme, of nuance and shade of meaning as you read the editorial originally? Had you read critically, you should have been. It's all there; nothing has been fabricated or distorted, nothing has been inferred or interposed that was not stated or clearly implied in the editorial as it appeared in the columns of the *Times*. If you missed it, you may need to read with much more critical sensitivity to the burden of meaning that resides within the printed word upon the page. If you missed it, you should resolve at once to practice sharpening your awareness of the full meaning and the complete thought, with its aura of connotative significance, of the words that you read. Every reader always does two things concomitantly: he reads for the literal meaning of the words; he also reads for implications, inferences, suggestions of meaning, and appreciations of the spirit of the word and the phrase. To read thus, to juggle two skills at one time so that the page may give up its fullest meaning and total beauty, this is to read critically. We have, of course, said nothing of the ineffable domain of poetry, where the beauty of language occurs in purest and most engaging form. But it is not the province of this little book to teach poetic appreciation. One suggestion may, however, be valuable. Read some poetry as a part of your general reading fare. Think of it not as something special—a type of reading that demands an "out-there" approach—but as something natural and as inexpressibly beautiful, as the stars or a flower. There is some "out-there" poetry; but if it means nothing to you, don't struggle with it. Read what appeals to you in poetry, and don't worry about your "aesthetic taste."

Read poetry as you would read prose: for the meaning. Ponder it, as you would ponder the marvels of nature: for their beauty and indescribable wonder of the thought expressed. As many a saint has travelled in beggar's weeds; just so, the divinest poetry is often expressed in ordinary prose. The editorial quoted above was in fact an ode to autumn, although it appeared amid the common prose of editorials addressed to the mundane issues of politics and the ephemeral happenings of the contemporary scene.

Poetry needs not the ministration of rhyme nor rhythm nor meter nor stanza in order to be. It needs only an alive and skillful reader who has the awareness to recognize the presence of beauty whenever and wherever he sees it—a beauty that often dwells amid the homely, ordinary words of the matter-of-fact page of print.

But the reader who sees it must read with his eyes wide open.

The appeal to spiritual and moral values. Man is an animal who is incurably religious. The appeal to man's spiritual aspirations and to his moral values is, therefore, one of the most basic and powerful of all appeals. Essentially, one's moral or spiritual values are the expression of life's best aspirations. They represent man yearning for perfection in an imperfect world, for a happy dream in the midst of a nightmare.

This urge takes many forms. It is expressed and suggested by a whole spectrum of synonyms—only a few of which may be mentioned here: good, right, excellent, just, fair, honest, sincere, straight, well-intentioned, generous, pure, unblemished—and the list might go on and on to great length.

Think how subtly these words are employed to condition your thinking and to influence your attitudes while reading. The daily paper arrives. You open it; and before your eyes is this full-page advertisement, with broad margins, suggestive of openness in generous proportions, and set in a type face which is clear, clean, and refined. It has all the marks of integrity and rectitude. It tells you:

> Fair play is our policy. Our business has been built on honest practices and a sincere desire to treat you right. For half a century, our business has been marked by an unblemished record of excellent customer relations. You will find our terms generous, our dealings just, our word good. Come in today for straight, well-intentioned advice with respect to your financial future.

Advertisements such as this are subtly powerful. They influence the reader's mind by capitalizing on a vocabulary which connotatively is high in the proportion of terms which suggest spiritual or moral values. Out of the twelve words given in the list of synonyms, eleven have been employed in that advertisement to connote conscientious practice of high moral standards. The appeal is to the reader's sense of the higher values of living. This does not mean to say that there is, per se, any insincerity in the advertisement or duplicity in intent. It merely points out the nature of the appeal.

But words may assume the piety of a monk while masking the thoughts of a rogue. For example, not long ago the following statement appeared in a newspaper advertisement in connection with a skill-building course:

> We can increase the efficiency of each student at least three times with equal or better comprehension of the subject as measured by beginning and final tests, or we will refund the student's entire tuition.

And so, having read that, you are perhaps willing to try something without risk. Either you come out three times better than you went in, or you get your money back. What have you to lose? It appears to be as simple as that: utterly honest, highly and scrupulously ethical. What could be more fair?

Now, *read* it.

Throw your mind in gear and engage your critical skills. And you will see that the seamless garb of integrity is full of holes!

"We can increase the efficiency of each student . . . ." That is a statement of possibility, not a promise. There is a vast difference between "we *can* increase" and "we *will* increase."

Let's go on. The next claim is a mathematical impossibility: "increase efficiency . . . at least three times." How can you multiply "efficiency" by three? You can multiply two by three; that's simple. And, furthermore, you can get an "answer." But to multiply "efficiency" by three is impossible.

It's like trying to measure twice as much love, or three times more courage.

But we continue: ". . . with equal or better comprehension of the subject." What does this mean? Equal or better than what? And what is "comprehension of the subject"? Again, the statement hangs in the verbal limbo of meaninglessness.

All right, you admit, that *is* a little vague; but the next phrase gives us solid ground on which to stand. Now we have a measure. The threefold increase in efficiency is to be measured by "initial and final tests." There, that is scientific! But is it? What kind of tests? Are the initial and final tests of comparable difficulty? Do they measure the same factors? Are they standardized tests? The statement does not say.

Even those of us who have attempted measurement of achievement with standardized tests—the most sophisticated of all educational measuring instruments—know that even they are not infallible. To use even these as a basis for refund of tuition might seem a somewhat shaky procedure.

Thus, what seems to be an honest guarantee of achievement or refund of tuition, what appears to be an altruistic gesture of generous magnanimity, turns out to be mere verbal obscurantism—foggy promises upon which return of tuition is predicated, the meaning of which can be neither established nor clarified.

The critical reader should be aware of verbal appeals such as these to moral, ethical, and spiritual values. These speak to the qualities of integrity and aspiration. There is much integrity and aspiration among us; there is also much exploitation in the name of integrity; and against this, the critical reader needs to be constantly on the *qui vive*.[2]

[2]Because this book deals with reading improvement, some of its readers may wish guidance with reference to professionally approved reading-improvement programs and diagnostic services. There are many of these throughout the country. Information has been included in the end-matter of this book as to ways in which these may be discovered, together with the professional Code of Ethics of the International Reading Association. You will find this material on pages 183–185.

Of the genuinely spiritual, of the truly moral and ethical literature every reader should know something. In a day when our world is becoming even more closely drawn together, when the barriers of race and clan are being crossed with ever-increasing ease, would it not be appropriate for the well-read adult to know something of the deepest aspirations and the greatest spiritual yearnings of all peoples of the earth. The Bible is the great spiritual and moral monument of the West, and we who are of Western thought and tradition should have read it. But as important as is the Bible to our own way of life, there are also comparable great and sacred writings of other peoples; and we can never understand these peoples until we appreciate their spiritual orientation, their moral code, and their philosophic viewpoint. *The Koran,* the *Bhagavad Gita,* the *Analects of Confucius,* the *Sutta-pitaka,* most of which are issued in paperback and can be found wherever paperbacks are sold, should be familiar to the well-read adult. For those who may wish the best of these between one set of covers, The Viking Press has issued a paperback, *The Portable World Bible,* edited by Robert O. Ballou. It is a valuable addition to any library, and it will give you an appreciation of the spiritual outlook of most of the world.

Reading with one's eyes wide open, then, means many things. It means that the reader must be awake to all the lures and stratagems that lie below the printed word and seek to influence the reader in one way or another. It means that you should be keenly aware of the meaning and the overtones of meaning. It implies that you should look, not only at the word, but through the word for implications, inferences, and nuances which, at first glance, may not lie open upon the surface of the page.

Rudolf Flesch, in *The Art of Clear Thinking,*[3] suggests a device that will reveal the subtlety of most of the appeals that authors make to readers. Dr. Flesch recommends two

[3] Rudolf Flesch, *The Art of Clear Thinking,* New York: Harper & Brothers, p. 69 ff.

simple tests. As you read, ask two questions of all statements: (1) So what? (2) Specify! These will bring to the surface the lurking artifices, the equivocation of verbal wolves that masquerade in sheep's clothing. These probes will demand that matters be put on the line so that both author and reader may operate in the open and have a clear and candid meeting of minds. These touchstones pierce the outside shell of verbal polish and reveal the intent within. They help readers to read with their eyes wide open.

7. And now, relax with a book and—read!

The purpose of learning to read is that you will read. Finally, this book will offer some suggestions for slippered reading in the easy chair. It will suggest ways in which you can build your own library and lay up for yourselves treasures upon your bookshelves that will serve you well all your days.

There is much to be said for a family devotion to books. Where children have been reared in the company of books and in the climate of reading and being read to, reading problems seldom occur. It is the home sterile of interest in books and reading that is the breeding ground for reading problems, retardation, and educational disability.

Reading should be a natural development within the family. Language should be entrancing for the child from the time he first hears it, and the wonder of it should never depart from him all the days of his years. The charm and fascination of words, the interesting thoughts of others, the argosies of treasure which no man can value—these all are the heritage and the gift of books.

For this reason, he who reads like an adult will also strive to live among books like an adult, gathering to himself those treasured and interesting volumes which he has purchased with his own hard-earned cash.

How to do this? Let the monthly newsletter of the Royal Bank of Canada advise you.

Building a Home Library[1]

Reading good books is not something to be indulged in as a luxury. It is a necessity for anyone who intends to give his life and work a touch of quality. The most real wealth is not what we put into our piggy banks but what we develop in our heads.

Books instruct us without anger, threats, and harsh discipline. They do not sneer at our ignorance or grumble at our mistakes. They ask only that we spend some time in the company of greatness so that we may absorb some of its attributes.

You do not read a book for the book's sake, but for your own.

You may read because in your high-pressure life, studded with problems and emergencies, you need periods of relief and yet recognize that peace of mind does not mean numbness of the soul.

You may read because you never had an opportunity to go to university, and books give you a chance to get something you missed.

You may read because your job is routine, and books give you a feeling of depth in life.

You may read because you see social, economic, and philosophical problems which need solution, and you believe that the best thinking of all past ages may be useful in your age, too.

You may read because you are tired of the shallowness of contemporary life, bored by the current conversational commonplaces, and wearied of shop talk and gossip about people.

Whatever your dominant personal reason, you will find that reading gives knowledge, creative power, satisfaction,

[1] "Building a Home Library," *The Royal Bank of Canada Monthly Letter*, Vol. 46, No. 8, August, 1965.

and relaxation. It cultivates your mind by calling its faculties into exercise.

It is well to have some destination in mind. As Arnold Bennett remarks in *Literary Taste* (a Pelican Book), a man starting out for a walk says to himself that he will reach some given point, or that he will progress at a given speed for a given distance, or that he will remain on his feet for a given time. He makes these decisions according to his ambition, his physical capacity, and his pleasure. So with reading.

Books are a source of pleasure the purest and the most lasting. They enhance your sensation of the interestingness of life. Reading them is not a violent pleasure like the gross enjoyment of an uncultivated mind, but a subtle delight.

Reading dispels prejudices which hem our minds within narrow spaces. One of the things that will surprise you as you read the Greek, Hebrew, and Christian books; the Roman, French, Italian, and British books; the books of philosophy, poetry, and politics; and the books that just tell about people having fun, is that human nature is much the same today as it has been ever since writing began to tell us about it.

Some people act as if it were demeaning to their manhood to wish to be well-read, but you can no more be a healthy person mentally without reading substantial books than you can be a vigorous person physically without eating solid food.

Perusal of good books will give you a mind of your own, bulwarked against the seduction of slogans. Through books you can escape from the ephemeral challenge of a crossword puzzle to the actual challenge of working out the why and wherefore of a segment of life. By borrowing the aid of a superior understanding you double your own understanding, meeting what the writer says with your personal thoughts.

The proper function of books is associated with intellectual culture in which you steer clear of generalities and indefinite views. You enlarge your critical sense regarding events and personalities and trends, so that you are no longer at the mercy of theorists and demagogues.

It is perfectly possible for a man, one who gives to reading only the leisure hours of a business life, to acquire such a general knowledge of the laws of nature and the facts of history that every great advance made in science and government and business shall be to him intelligible and interesting.

Choosing books. In deciding what books to read and what books to have in your private library, you need to take a wide sweep. There is a book to match your mood whatever it may be. There are books that are gentle and quieting, and books that are exciting and inspiring. All that mankind has done and thought, gained and lost: it is lying as in magic preservation in the pages of books. You should have a good selection of them within arm's reach.

As you read, your taste will become trained so as to increase your capacity for pleasure, enabling you to enter into a great variety of experiences. It will reject books that are fifth-rate, fraudulent, and meretricious. You will not allow trash in books' clothing into your library.

You will, of course, have utility books on your shelves. There are some books which one must read if he is to progress in his job. The man who depends only upon his own experience is confined to narrow limits both of place and time. Non-readers are seldom remarkable for the exactness of their learning or the breadth of their thinking.

When you come to choose the general books for your library, you may be torn between buying new books and buying old books. The good books of the hour, like the good books of all time, contain useful or pleasant talk of some person with whom you cannot otherwise converse. They can be very useful often, telling you what you need to know; very pleasant often, as a personal friend's talk would be.

They may be bright accounts of travel, good-humored and witty discussions of events, lively or pathetic story-telling, or firm fact-reporting by men and women concerned in the events of passing history.

Perhaps the problem of old and new may be solved in this way: if you have not read a book before, it is to all intents and purposes new to you whether it was printed yesterday or three centuries ago. Apply the tests of appropriateness, taste, and truth; and you can read ancient or modern with assurance.

Read great books. Whatever you read, read "greats." A great book is one that, shining through time and space, lights our lives, illuminating depths within us we were not conscious of. It is one of the great thrills of life to uncover thoughts we did not know we were capable of having.

All the greatest books contain food for all ages, and have things of consequence to say to us here and now.

There is no positive hierarchy among books, but we cannot go wrong when we peruse masterpieces. These are not designed to rouse your admiration but to wake up your mind and spirit.

"A classic," Mark Twain said, "is something everybody wants to have read and nobody wants to read." The word "classical" applied to books or music simply means what has worn best. The consent of the ages has marked them out for all time.

Why are the classics so often recommended? Arnold Bennett wrote in *Literary Taste:* "You are not in a position to choose among modern works. To sift the wheat from the chaff is a process that takes an exceedingly long time. Modern works have to pass before the bar of the taste of successive generations. Whereas, with classics, *your* taste has to pass before the bar of the classics."

Reading the classics is not to worship at the shrine of antiquity. We do not wish to look at life through the eyes of dead Greeks, but what those eyes saw of life is of help in interpreting what is going on today.

Making a list. So here you are at the crucial question: what sort of books shall I read? You cannot sail through the sea of books like a ship without pilot or rudder.

No single person is fitted to declare which are the hundred or thousand best books, but it is worthwhile to look at the lists that great men in art, science, business, education, and statesmanship have made as their choices.

It is evident from these lists that whether our reading be great or small it should be general. If the demands of making a living leave only a short time for reading, that is all the more reason why our reading should remind us of the vast expanse of human thought and the wonderful variety of human nature.

Do not go overboard about one author or one subject, however exalted. You can become a bore if you read too much of one kind of stuff. You may tire your companions to death with dinosaurs, if you read exclusively about the Mesozoic period; or you may jade your friends by falling into poses and speech of the characters in Dickens' novels if they become your specialty.

Judicious reading should leave no great type of thought, no dominant phase of human nature, wholly a blank. St. John's College, in Annapolis, Maryland, has built its course of study around some hundred great books. They make strange shelf-fellows. They include saints (Augustine and Aquinas); a thief (François Villon); the first war correspondent (Herodotus); a surgeon (Galen); a statesman (Cicero); a revolutionist (Marx); a traveller (Homer); a playwright (Euripides); scientists (Aristotle, Newton, Einstein); philosophers (Socrates, Kant, Plato); an artist (Leonardo); and novelists (Tolstoy, Flaubert, Fielding, Thackeray).

Fortunately, nobody can pick your books for you. You have to do it yourself, fitting them to your needs and desires.

Any general list of books to read must necessarily be arbitrary, but there are several guides to start your thinking. There is a book called *Have You Read 100 Great Books?* (Jasper Lee Company, New York), which provides in its 144 pages fifty lists of books, ancient and modern, every one prepared by a respected figure in literature, history, science, or education.

Selection is helped by several paperbacks: *The Lifetime Reading Plan* by Clifton Fadiman (Avon); *Books That Changed the World* by Robert B. Downs (Mentor); *Much Loved Books* by James O'Donnell Bennett (Premier); *Highlights of Modern Literature* (Mentor).[2]

From these you may make a list of books you wish to own. Then visit the book stores and the second-hand book stores regularly with your list in hand. When you find a book that is on your list, at a price you wish to pay, buy it. Then your library will be truly hand-picked, special to you.

One man who did not wish to be bound by any ready-made catalogue prepared his own book and reading list in this way: he adapted the Dewey Decimal Classification System, which was originated by Melvil Dewey, to serve as a method that would index books. The numbers you see on the backs of library books are likely Dewey numbers: "025.8" indicates to the librarian that the book so marked is about library administration and has special reference to book arrangement and preservation.

The Dewey System has ten classes, every one divided and sub-divided many times. The classes are: 000 General works, 100 Philosophy, 200 Religion, 300 Social sciences, 400 Philol-

[2] Another title which the *Letter* might well have included is *The College and Adult Reading List of Books in Literature and the Fine Arts,* prepared by the Committee on College and Adult Reading List, National Council of Teachers of English (a Washington Square Press Book), 1962.—author's note.

ogy, 500 Pure science, 600 Applied science, 700 Arts and recreation, 800 Literature, 900 History.

Covering the field of knowledge. In pursuit of a general reading plan to cover all fields of knowledge, you make sure that you obtain books in every class. Then you follow through the classes in order, reading a book in each.

You may read Henry David Thoreau's essay on "Civil Disobedience" and recall that from it Mahatma Gandhi derived his passive disobedience régime. When Dr. Will Durant's *Story of Philosophy* was published in 1926 it leaped to immediate popularity which has continued through the years. It does not teach you philosophy, but it does provide a chart of the province of philosophy and leads you into many entrancing books in which the writers discuss hopes and doubts that present themselves with undiminished interest to every man and woman.

You will enjoy and profit by the *Meditations* of Marcus Aurelius, his dispassionate gravity, his noble forgetfulness of self, his tenderness toward others. You will enjoy applying the *Discourses* of Epictetus to modern life as one suburban Montreal group did a few years ago. There are surprisingly many chapters which can be read as of today, though they were written in the first century.

When you come to the "200" class you will read the *Bible* freshly like a book, not droningly and dully. This is made simple in *The Bible Designed to Be Read as Living Literature.* The King James Version is retained as to text, but the type is clear and easily read, the poems are set out as poetry, and the drama as drama. Every great religion has its own books, and all are worth dipping into for their revelation of the way people in all ages have satisfied their need for spiritual expression.[3]

---

[3] See page 145 for reference to *The Portable World Bible,* ed. Robert O. Ballou (Viking).

When you come to science, a good book with which to start is *Science and the Modern World* by Alfred North Whitehead (Macmillan, 1926; Pelican, 1938). He takes you from the first century of modern science, starting in 1600, to this century's rejection of preconceived ideas and acceptance of an open-minded search for secure foundations.

In the social sciences you will find books which started great human movements, books like *Capital* by Karl Marx and *The Age of Reason* by Thomas Paine.

In the 800 class you will read the great dramas: *Agamemnon* and *Oedipus Rex* and *Hamlet* and *King Lear* and *Peer Gynt*, which transcend all factual statement in their illumination of the dark complexity of human dilemmas and the ambiguity of human behavior.

If you start your reading of history with Wells' *Outline of History* you obtain not only an over-all view of the story of mankind from the beginning up to recent years, but an introduction to many fascinating byways to be explored through other books.

When planning your history reading, do not omit your own country. *The New York Times* said in its 1865 review of Francis Parkman's latest book about French pioneers in the New World: "He writes like a scholar and a gentleman, and all who have read his *History of the Conspiracy of Pontiac* —probably the most thorough and complete historical account of a single separate act in the great drama of European civilization that our literature has seen—will be glad to meet him in the more extended field of investigation opened out in this elegant volume" (*France and England in North America*).

Marc Lescarbot, who wrote the drama, *The Theatre of Neptune*, which was presented at Port Royal in 1606 as Canada's first theatrical performance, was also an historian. He published an entertaining account of the discoveries in the

New World under the title, *Histoire de la Nouvelle France.*
An edition in English was published by the Champlain Society in Toronto.

How to read. It is obvious that reading is not refined idle-
ness. The person who hopes to make something worth while
out of his reading cannot afford to disport himself in the
flowery pastures of frivolous and trivial literature. It is le-
gitimate to read a book for no other reason than to divert
your mind from a troublesome idea, but it need not be a
sleazy book.

It is impossible to give any method to our pursuit of
the best till we get nerve enough to reject the weeds that
threaten to overgrow our little patch of fruit-bearing reading.

You will find it unprofitable to approach a book with a
blank mind and passive understanding, as one enters a cocktail party. Between these covers are thoughts worthy of your
attention, ideas to solve your problems, inspiration that may
enlighten your life. You have seen a child turning the pages
of a Christmas catalogue, his eyes sparkling in anticipation of
the new things to be seen. That is the sort of expectancy you
should bring to your books.

Read boldly and in an unprejudiced way. Francis Bacon
wrote: "Some books are to be tasted, others to be swallowed,
and some few to be chewed and digested." Passive perusing
may be all very well for escape stories, but it won't do at
all for books which can improve one's mind, stir one's ambi-
tions, pacify one's perturbations.

Some people are deterred from attempting what are regarded as stiff books for fear they should not understand
them, but it is wise and stimulating to read close to the upper limits of your mental powers. Your mind is probably
capable of more than you think, if only you press it somewhat,
and accept the challenge of something a little difficult.

When you have your own books you can make reading easier, remembering more certain, and review quicker, if you read with pencil in hand. It is a poor objection to say "it would spoil the book," for you did not buy the book as a dealer to sell it again, but as a scholar. Intelligent marking gives a kind of abstract to the book, picking out the key sentences.[4]

Your family library. There are few hobbies more satisfying than the gradual collecting of good books.

Possession of books does not give knowledge, but it does make knowledge readily available. You may sit in a small home library and see the endless procession of human thought and passion and action as it passes. Even to build some shelves before you begin to stock books gives you exhilaration and excitement, because on those shelves you are going to place books that will become part of your intellectual life and that of your family.

When you have a number of selected books, you do not need to decide beforehand what friends you will invite to spend the evening with you. When supper is over and you sit down for your hour of companionship with the great writers, you give your invitation according to your inclination at the time. And if you have made a mistake, and the friend is, after all, not the one you want to talk with, you can "shut him up" without hurting his feelings. These are friends who speak only when you want to listen, and keep silent when you want to think.

It may not suit the décor of your living-room to have shelves full of books there. But books are accommodating in this regard also: they can be stacked anywhere. E. M. Forster, author of *A Passage to India*, said that he had books

[4]See Paul D. Leedy, *Read with Speed and Precision*, (McGraw-Hill, 1963), pages 47–48, 95, for additional suggestions in the marking of books.

not only in his library but in his bedroom, in his sittingroom, and in a bathroom cupboard.

A library is not to be regarded as a solemn chamber, but may be some small snug corner, perhaps in the cellar, almost entirely walled in by books. It is a place where you go to take counsel with all that have been wise and great and good and glorious among the men who have gone before you. It is pleasant to sit down in that corner just being aware that these authors, with their accumulated wisdom and charm, are waiting for you to open a conversation.

Building such a personal library is not an expensive undertaking. Millions of people have discovered books during the past thirty years through the book clubs and the paperback editions. Included are some of the very best books ever written.[5]

No matter how tight your budget strings may be pulled, Shakespeare and Toynbee and Franklin and Whitehead and Socrates and Santayana and Churchill and Durant will visit you. They come dressed in faded leather from the second-hand book store or in paper from the up-to-date book dealer and the railway news stand, at the cost of less than a dollar each. They represent, whether dressed in the brilliant finery of dust-covers or in ragged buckram, the world's accumulated hoard of mellow beauty and practical wisdom.

Children deserve such a library. Homes with no books, parents who read only the daily paper and an occasional magazine, have a negative influence upon the intellectual development of children.

Do not waste time in deciding what books to provide for your children: start giving them some of the best within their

[5] A convenient guide to *any* paperback title is a work which is available at any bookseller or public library: *Paperback Books in Print*. As its title indicates, it lists every paperback book in print in English in three ways: by author, by title, and by subject area.

understanding. Books should be chosen, not for their freedom from evil, but for their possession of good. Dr. Johnson said: "Whilst you stand deliberating which book your son shall read first, another boy has read both."

Read and stock no mean books, but those which exalt and inspire. Literature exists so that where one man has lived finely thousands may afterwards learn to live finely. Reading a good book makes you feel warm and comfortable inside you. Your mind is cultivating appreciation of the excellent.

Self-evaluation section: test your skills and abilities

How Alert Are You?

This is a test of your alertness while reading. Do not refer back to the paragraphs of the selection which you have just read. Check the choice which you feel to be the correct one.

1. Which of the following phrases did you notice as you read the selection did not seem to fit logically with the meaning? (a) problem solving, (b) bootless wrangle, (c) willing to concede, (d) problem causing, (e) problem situation.

2. Which two of the following marks of punctuation attracted your attention because they were incorrectly used? (a) . (b) , (c) : (d) ? (e) ; (f) " " (g) ! (h) 's (i) ( ) (j) —

3. The main idea of this selection was stated twice during your reading. Which of the following states the main idea? (a) Efficient executives maintain harmonious personnel relations between employer and employees; (b) Problems involving personnel dissatisfaction can usually be resolved by providing the overworked employee with more help; (c) Big problems usually result from little problems that are not given proper attention; (d) Solving a problem begins by disentangling the problem from the problem situation; (e) Problem solvers are sometimes blamed for situations over which they have no control.

4. What incongruity did you notice in the reading of this selection? (a) The selection begins with one main idea and ends with

another; (b) The reasoning is faulty; (c) The example begins with one character and ends with another; (d) The example is inappropriate to the main idea; (e) The whole situation is unrelated to a practical life situation.

Now, check your answers for correctness against those given in the Answer Key found on page 186. Enter your score for alertness here:

Number correct (____) × 20 = ____%

Rate of Reading

You timed yourself on this selection. Find your rate of reading from the following table:

Minutes	Seconds	Words per Minute	Minutes	Seconds	Words per Minute
0	30	494	1	20	186
0	35	424	1	25	175
0	40	371	1	30	165
0	45	329	1	35	156
0	50	297	1	40	148
0	55	270	1	50	135
1	00	247	2	00	124
1	05	228	2	10	114
1	10	212	2	20	106
1	15	196	2	30	99

How Accurately Do You Recall What You Have Read?

This is a test on the section on Recall which you have just finished reading. Answer the questions below without referring to the text.

1. To illustrate a point in the discussion, the situation was given of your meeting a new acquaintance while walking down the street with your friend. He introduces you and says, "John, meet_____. (Write in the name of the person to whom you were introduced.)

2. You find you are both mountain climbers, and he says, "Call me sometime," and gives you his telephone exchange and number. What number does he tell you to call? _____.

3. You were given three steps to greater memory power. Jot these down as nearly verbatim as you can:

(a)_____

(b)_____

(c)_____

4. The section on Recall opened with an adage. Quote it:

_____

5. To what is the forgetting of facts compared?

_____

6. What can "boost your recall ability to new heights"?

_____

Check your answers for correctness. Turn to the Answer Key, page 186. Enter your score for Recall Ability here:

Number correct (____) × 12.5 = ____%

Near-Vision Test (Reading Vision)

This is, of course, a very gross screening test, but it may give you some indication of your visual adequacy. Reproduced on the next page, through the courtesy of the Guild of Prescription Opticians of America, is a near-vision test card. Hold the card 14 inches from your eyes. What is the last line of print that you can read clearly and easily? You should be able to read to at least within one line from the bottom of the card (i.e. the line which has the 95% above it in the extreme right-hand column). If you cannot read easily the lines with the 90% above them, it may indicate the need to consult an ophthalmologist or an optometrist for a visual examination.

Jot down here the percentage of near-visual efficiency (the figures in the extreme right-hand column) above the line which you could read with ease:

How efficiently do you see?................____%

NEAR VISION TEST CARD

UNIVERSITY OF LOUISVILLE

REVISED JAEGER STANDARD	NEAR SNELLEN NOTATION	METRIC DISTANCE	DISTANCE SNELLEN APPROXIMATION	DECIMAL NOTATION	A. M. A. 1955 NEAR VISUAL EFFICIENCY
12	14/89 (in.)	2.25 M.	20/130 (ft.)	0.15	10%

WHEN IN THE COURSE OF HUMAN EVENTS, IT BECOMES NECESSARY FOR

11	14/79	2.0	20/120	0.2	13%

ONE PEOPLE TO DISSOLVE THE POLITICAL BANDS WHICH HAVE CONNECTED THEM

9	14/60	1.5	20/85	0.22	20%

WITH ANOTHER, AND TO ASSUME AMONG THE POWERS OF THE EARTH, THE SEPARATE AND EQUAL STATION TO

7	14/42	1.05	20/60	0.35	40%

WHICH THE LAWS OF NATURE AND OF NATURE'S GOD ENTITLE THEM. A DECENT RESPECT TO THE OPINIONS OF MANKIND REQUIRES THAT THEY SHOULD DECLARE THE

6	14/35	.82	20/50	0.4	50%

CAUSES WHICH IMPEL THEM TO THE SEPARATION. WE HOLD THESE TRUTHS TO BE SELF-EVIDENT. THAT ALL MEN ARE CREATED EQUAL. THAT THEY ARE ENDOWED BY THEIR CREATOR WITH CERTAIN UNALIENABLE

5	14/28	.75	20/40	0.5	90%

RIGHTS, THAT AMONG THESE ARE LIFE, LIBERTY, AND THE PURSUIT OF HAPPINESS. THAT TO SECURE THESE RIGHTS, GOVERNMENTS ARE INSTITUTED AMONG MEN, DERIVING THEIR JUST POWERS FROM THE CONSENT OF THE GOVERNED,

3	14/21	.53	20/30	0.6	95%

THAT WHENEVER ANY FORM OF GOVERNMENT BECOMES DESTRUCTIVE OF THESE ENDS. IT IS THE RIGHT OF THE PEOPLE TO ALTER OR TO ABOLISH IT. AND TO INSTITUTE NEW GOVERNMENT. LAYING ITS FOUNDATION ON SUCH PRINCIPLES AND ORGANIZING ITS POWERS IN SUCH FORM. AS TO THEM SHALL SEEM MOST LIKELY TO

1	14/14	.37	20/20	1.0	100%

EFFECT THEIR SAFETY AND HAPPINESS. PRUDENCE. INDEED. WILL DICTATE THAT GOVERNMENTS LONG ESTABLISHED SHOULD NOT BE CHANGED FOR LIGHT AND TRANSIENT CAUSES. AND ACCORDINGLY ALL EXPERIENCE HATH SHOWN. THAT MANKIND ARE MORE DISPOSED TO SUFFER. WHILE EVILS ARE SUFFERABLE. THAN TO RIGHT THEMSELVES BY ABOLISHING THE FORMS TO WHICH THEY ARE ACCUSTOMED. BUT WHEN A LONG TRAIN OF ABUSES AND USURPATIONS.

CHART TO BE HELD
14 INCHES FROM EYE

ENGINEERED AND PRODUCED BY
COURIER-JOURNAL LITHO CO., LOUISVILLE 18, KY.

Do You Have Astigmatism?

Hold this page at reading distance (14–16 inches from the eyes). Look at the circle below first with one eye closed, then the other. Are there pie-shaped sections that seem sharper, blacker than others? Check the correct box: ☐ Yes ☐ No

If you checked the "yes" box, astigmatism (a distortion caused by an imperfect curvature of the eye's optical surfaces) may be indicated. The condition is quite common—and easily corrected.

Of course, this is no proper eye test. Only a professional eye examination can confirm whatever you seem to discover in this test. In fact, only by a professional eye examination every year or so can you be sure you're seeing as well as you should.

How Large Is Your Word-Hoard?

Here is an opportunity to test your word power. All of the words in this list have been used thus far in the chapter. Check the word or expression which means most nearly the same as the first (master) word.

1. adage: (a) something additional, (b) the present age, (c) an established saying, (d) an allusion, (e) an illusion

2. apathetic: (a) opposed, (b) choleric, (c) splenetic, (d) phlegmatic, (e) sanguine

3. augur: (a) to bore, (b) to predict, (c) to write, (d) to look, (e) to seek

4. avid: (a) eager, (b) dry, (c) mad, (d) noncommittal, (e) apathetic

5. category: (a) mangled cat, (b) catenary, (c) classification, (d) flood, (e) waterfall

6. connote: (a) denote, (b) notate, (c) annotate, (d) suggest, (e) clarify

7. fleetness: (a) group of vessels, (b) wool, (c) celerity, (d) celery, (e) type of cloud

8. fortuitous: (a) defending, (b) inherited, (c) evil, (d) unknown, (e) accidental

9. genie: (a) bad luck, (b) attendant spirit, (c) evil eye, (d) ghost, (e) species

10. incidental: (a) beginning, (b) inceptive, (c) casual, (d) quick, (e) slow

11. militate: (a) march, (b) encamp, (c) enlist, (d) wage war, (e) affect

12. nonchalant: (a) indifferent, (b) unequal, (c) unintelligent, (d) undivided, (e) nondescript

13. nuance: (a) slight gradation, (b) musical note, (c) ninth hour, (d) gradient, (e) graduation

14. ogling: (a) casting remarks, (b) casting aspersion, (c) casting doubt, (d) casting glances, (e) castigating

15. omnibus: (a) all-inclusive, (b) all filled, (c) all-transporting, (d) all-carrying, (e) all united

16. onus: (a) musical composition, (b) obligation, (c) extra money, (d) gift, (e) book

17. peripheral: (a) internal, (b) external, (c) central, (d) under side, (e) top side
18. potential: (a) possibility, (b) ruler, (c) strength, (d) rheostat, (e) dose
19. *qui vive:* (a) alive, (b) alert, (c) alone, (d) aloof, (e) *a la mode*
20. rationale: (a) food alotted to each person, (b) the intelligence, (c) underlying reason, (d) analysis of personality, (e) relationship
21. shore: (a) prop, (b) hand, (c) sink, (d) swell, (e) stand
22. *sine qua non:* (a) a curve, (b) a necessity, (c) an indefinite date, (d) a legal proceeding, (e) a nonentity
23. subtle: (a) dishonest, (b) tricky, (c) spurious, (d) crafty, (e) artless
24. trivia: (a) three-legged stand, (b) three liberal arts, (c) three-pronged fork, (d) trifles, (e) trash
25. vigilant: (a) sleepy, (b) proud, (c) watchful, (d) manly, (e) poisonous

Now, check your answers for correctness. Refer to the Answer Key, page 186. Enter your score, which will indicate your word-hoard, here: Number correct (____) × 4 = ____%

How Well Do You Sense Structure?

The chapter which you have just read has a clear structure and organization. Below are several outline patterns. Select the one which represents the structure of the chapter.

I	II	III	IV
A. _____	A. _____	A. _____	A. _____
1. _____	B. _____	B. _____	1. _____
2. _____	C. _____	1. _____	2. _____
a. ___	1. _____	2. _____	3. _____
b. ___	2. _____	a. ___	4. _____
B. _____	3. _____	b. ___	B. _____
C. _____	D. _____	c. ___	C. _____
D. _____	E. _____	3. _____	D. _____
1. _____	1. _____	4. _____	1. _____
2. _____	2. _____	5. _____	2. _____
		C. _____	3. _____

Now, check the correctness of your answer with the Answer Key, page 187.

And Now, Draw Your Profile . . .

On the next page is an evaluation scale of your reading strengths and weaknesses. This chapter began with the question, Do you have what it takes to read well? Now, let's find out. Plot your scores on the scale at the appropriate points. Connect the score locations. What does it tell you?

If any of your placements fall in the shadow zone, you should give special attention to these areas, trying to improve them.

How Keen Is Your Sense of Acuteness and Awareness in Reading Paragraphs?

(Do not refer back to any part of the chapter which you have just read while testing your skills on these questions.)

I. Below is the section which you have just read on pages 47–48. In the following version, however, all of the cue words from the original text have been deleted. In each place where one of these words originally occurred, a caret ($\wedge$) has been inserted in the line.

Supply above each caret, between the lines, the appropriate orientational word or words which will indicate clearly the proper thought relationship. Use as many varied expressions as necessary to keep the reader thoroughly and accurately oriented as to what is happening with the thought.

You may also insert additional carets and cue words to those already indicated as $_\wedge$we have done in this sentence. To do so may, *[for example]* however, affect the smoothness of the style; but do not let this con-

Your Reading Aptitude Profile

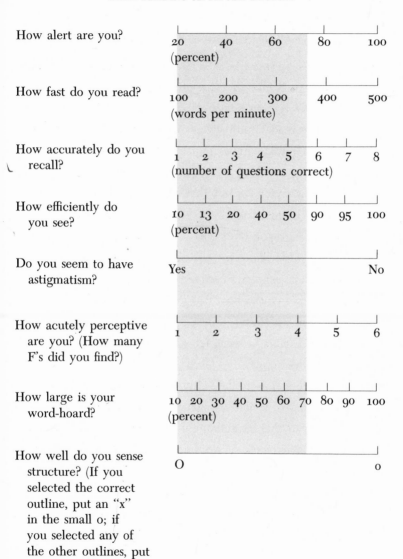

How alert are you?

20   40   60   80   100
(percent)

How fast do you read?

100   200   300   400   500
(words per minute)

How accurately do you recall?

1   2   3   4   5   6   7   8
(number of questions correct)

How efficiently do you see?

10   13   20   40   50   90   95   100
(percent)

Do you seem to have astigmatism?

Yes   No

How acutely perceptive are you? (How many F's did you find?)

1   2   3   4   5   6

How large is your word-hoard?

10   20   30   40   50   60   70   80   90   100
(percent)

How well do you sense structure? (If you selected the correct outline, put an "x" in the small o; if you selected any of the other outlines, put an "x" in the large o.)

O   o

cern you. The purpose of this exercise is to test your awareness of the need for orientational words and to employ them to indicate to the reader as many relationships of the thought as possible.

Not Everything Is a Paragraph That Looks Like One

A   [1] Appearances are deceptive. [2]∧Authors are whimsical. [3]∧Not everything *is* a paragraph that looks like one.

B   [1] The reader must always be in command. [2] In facing a page of print,∧nothing replaces the agile, active, inquiring, analyzing mind of a reader who knows exactly what the author is saying because that reader knows exactly what the author is doing with the thought and precisely what is transpiring upon the page.

C   ([1] *Incidentally, have you been in command?* [2]∧*Has the somewhat complex structure of the thought in the last two paragraphs eluded you?* [3] *At the close of this section you will have an opportunity to test your "command status," so that you will want to keep alert from here on.* [4] *Watch for reading booby traps.*)

D   [1] Indentations in the left margin of print usually signal the beginning of a new thought. [2]∧This is not always true. [3] It may mean∧that the author is merely providing "reader relief."

E   [1]∧Great blocks of print are depressing to many readers. [2] They see them as ponderous and forbidding. [3]∧Authors know this. [4] They sometimes break up a longer discussion into subdiscussions—as we have been doing in this chapter with this rather extended discussion of the paragraph—or perhaps an extended paragraph into subparagraphs.

F [1] Reasons∧may be detached from the facts which they logically justify. [2]∧Examples may be separated by paragraph division from the principles which they illustrate. [3] Logically ∧these should be in the same prose package with the material with which they are inseparably linked. [4]∧This may form inordinately long discussions and paragraph structures which, because of their very length, may have adverse psychological effects on the reader.

G [1] It is psychologically advantageous∧occasionally to separate integrally connected parts of a discussion,∧to do so places a greater burden upon your reading skill and ability, your acuteness and sense of awareness of what is happening on the page.

II. In paragraph A, which of the following arrangements (according to the number assigned to each sentence) indicates the way the sentences *should* be arranged so that they will be in the most logical sequence? Circle the group of your choice.

1,2,3; 1,3,2; 2,3,1; 2,1,3; 3,2,1; 3,1,2.

III. In the above selection, if the integrity of the thought is preserved, two paragraphs should be incorporated into one longer paragraph. Write in the blanks the letters of the paragraphs which ought to be thus consolidated:

_____ and _____

Why have you made this choice? Explain:_____

_____

_____

IV. Assume that you are editing the section reprinted above. If so, you might divide it into subsections according to the structure of the thought. Also, each of the subsections has a "master" paragraph (a paragraph which enunciates the main idea of the section).

Indicate in the blanks below: (1) the letter designations of the paragraphs which you would bracket into each subsection; (2) the paragraph in each subsection which you consider to be the master paragraph, by circling the letter designation; and (3) the editorial caption, or heading, which you would give each section. Be brief and precise.

Paragraph Letter
Designation   Editorial Caption

_____   _____

_____   _____

Now, check the correctness of your answers with the Answer Key, pages 188–190.

How Large Is Your Word-Hoard—Now?

In Chapter 1, you had an opportunity to assess your vocabulary resources. The words in that test were taken from the first chapter of the book. Now, you are about to begin a new chapter. From Chapter 3, the following twenty words have been selected. You will encounter these as you read the chapter. Test yourself now on your vocabulary resources for reading the chapter—*before* you begin. Check the word or phrase among the choices given which means the same, or nearly the same as the master word.

1. agile: (a) languid, (b) protracted, (c) regressive, (d) magical, (e) deft
2. categorical: (a) having curvilinear qualities, (b) chainlike, (c) relating to teaching by questioning, (d) absolute, (e) symbolical
3. celerity: (a) vegetable, (b) speed, (c) famous person, (d) unmarried person, (e) quality or shape of cells
4. cope: (a) stake, (b) give, (c) go away, (d) contend, (e) contaminate
5. delve: (a) descend, (b) ascend, (c) reveal, (d) dig, (e) plant
6. dexterity: (a) type of sugar, (b) sleight of hand, (c) adroitness, (d) a drug, (e) a clown

7. ensconce: (a) to fit a candle into a holder, (b) to place securely, (c) to provide plenteously, (d) to see clearly, (e) to act cleverly

8. expedite: (a) to turn over a criminal to authorities, (b) to cast out, (c) to facilitate, (d) to prevent from going, (e) to send best wishes

9. format: (a) a type of floor covering, (b) form and arrangement, (c) type of mold, (d) key or guide, (e) general situation.

10. gist: (a) summary, (b) grain, (c) ghost, (d) blast of wind, (e) visitor

11. instanter: (a) request, (b) short space of time, (c) at once, (d) electronic relay device, (e) one who stands in for another person

12. orientation: (a) act of becoming adjusted, (b) decoration, (c) a type of rug weaving, (d) Chinese art work, (e) gold ore

13. peripheral: (a) pertaining to a type of fever, (b) relating to medicine, (c) marginal, (d) abbreviated, (e) scornful

14. pragmatic: (a) breaking into pieces, (b) skilled, (c) equivalent, (d) injurious, (e) practical

15. precipitous: (a) sheer, (b) resembling a sediment, (c) falling down, (d) pertaining to a geologic era, (e) disintegrating

16. premise: (a) a pledge, (b) a first performance, (c) a reward, (d) an animal, (e) an assumption

17. rationale: (a) fundamental reason, (b) supply of provisions, (c) the act of reasoning, (d) a fixed allowance, (e) relation of one thing to another

18. static: (a) electrical, (b) pertaining to a radio, (c) by-product of lightning, (d) stationary, (e) interfering

19. verbiage: (a) weeds, (b) wordiness, (c) vegetation, (d) word-for-word order, (e) forbidden

20. vicarious: (a) having to do with the clergy, (b) in the vicinity of, (c) wicked, (d) taking the place of another, (e) decayed

Now, check your answers for correctness. Refer to the Answer Key, page 191. Enter your score, which will indicate your word-hoard now:

Number correct (____) × 5 = ____%

Punctuation Makes All the Difference

Recently, Maxwell Nurnberg has been running in *Pleasures in Learning,* a publication of the Division of General Education and Extension Services of New York University, some punctuation puzzlers. Through the kindness of Mr. Nurnberg, permission was granted to reprint some of these here, so that you may test your aptness with punctuation.[1] When finished, check your answers with those on page 191.

1. A sign reads: PRIVATE
                        NO SWIMMING
                           ALLOWED

   Punctuate this so that it grants permission to go swimming.

2. (a) Thirteen girls knew the secret, all told.
   (b) Thirteen girls knew the secret; all told.
          (Which is a libel on the fair sex?)

3. (a) I left him convinced he was a fool.
   (b) I left him, convinced he was a fool.
          (Which sentence shows extraordinary powers of persuasion?)

4. (a) The butler was asked to stand by the door and call the guests names as they arrived.
   (b) The butler was asked to stand by the door and call the guests' names as they arrived.
          (Which may result in an embarrassing situation?)

5. (a) A pretty young salesgirl waited on me.
   (b) A pretty, young salesgirl waited on me.
          (By which salesgirl would you rather be waited on?)

6. (a) Go slow—children.
   (b) Go slow, children.
          (Which is a warning to drivers?)

[1] Maxwell Nurnberg, *Punctuation Pointers,* New York: Scholastic Publications, 1967. Reprinted by permission.

7. (a) Senate Group Eats Chickens, Cabinet Wives, Sweetbreads.
   (b) Senate Group Eats Chickens; Cabinet Wives, Sweetbreads.
       (Which headline is the more cannibalistic?)

8. (a) What great scientist recently wrote an article beginning with the three-word sentence, "I am frightened"?
   (b) What great scientist recently wrote an article beginning with the three-word sentence, "I am frightened?"
       (In which sentence does the scientist imply that he is not frightened?)

9. (a) Population of New York City Broken Down by Age and Sex
   (b) Population of New York City, Broken Down by Age and Sex
       (Which headline is unfair to 8,000,000 people?)

10. (a) She, too, eagerly awaits the spring.
    (b) She too eagerly awaits the spring.
        (Which is a neurotic personality?)

How Well-Formed Are Your Reading Habits?

(Reading Habit Test)

DIRECTIONS: Place a check mark in the column which describes the frequency with which you practice each of the following habits or attitudes.

	Never	Rarely	Sometimes	Usually	Always
1. I accept the fact that improvement in reading is largely a personal responsibility directly related to my own effort and alertness, so that I try to stay alert, observe keenly, and note facts in precise detail.° (1–22)					
2. I know I can read better if I really try, and so whenever I read I always try to improve my reading. (85–86)					

° If you wish to refer to the part of the book where this matter was discussed, the numbers in parentheses following the item indicate the pages on which you will find the discussion.

	Never	Rarely	Sometimes	Usually	Always

3. I set aside some time every day for the express purpose of improving my reading skills. (2)

4. When I read, I am consciously alert to the thought of the author, the features of the page, and the subtle nuances of word meanings. (4–6)

5. I recall facts, names, minutiae readily and accurately. (7–10)

6. I can read for long periods of time without a feeling of eye fatigue or general tiredness. (13)

7. I feel adequate in my ability to express in words any idea which may occur to me.* (16–17)

8. I have known readily the meaning of every word in this book thus far so that I could unhesitatingly give a synonym for it. (17–19)

9. I consciously size up a page (or a set of pages) before beginning to read it (them), to look for any distinguishing features which will aid me in reading. (23–27)

10. As I read, I am aware of the presence of the paragraph and the structure of it. (29–34)

11. In reading a paragraph I look for the main idea, and then I am conscious of the function of each sentence in developing the main thought. (34–35)

* If you wish to test your ability on this one, turn to pages 166 and 172. There you will find a test on words taken from preceding chapters.

	Never	Rarely	Sometimes	Usually	Always

12. I immediately notice "dud" sentences in a paragraph. (35–36)

13. I notice immediately the directional words within a paragraph and their effect on the development of the thought. (38–46)

14. When reading, I am immediately aware of "half paragraphs" and "double paragraphs." (47–48)

15. When I read, I am acutely aware of the structuralization of the thought either in outline or by some other specific structuralized pattern. (48–50)

16. As I read, I am alert to the function of punctuation in helping to make the writing meaningful. (51–69)

17. I specifically look for the possibility of short cuts in reading. (71–85)

18. I define in my own thinking the pur-. pose for which I am reading. (73–74)

19. I am always aware of the need to read rapidly, yet I am equally aware that speed is not all-important in every reading situation. (74)

20. Before reading an extended passage I flip the pages to look analytically at the material to be read. (77–79)

21. I make it a habit to skim the article by reading only the main ideas before I read the material in greater detail. (79–80)

	Never	Rarely	Sometimes	Usually	Always

22. I read only so far as I need to read to satisfy my purpose, omitting whatever is unrewarding or needless. (80–81)

23. I read telegraphically, by noting only the essential words. (81)

24. I am alert to all graphic devices and seek their message directly. (82–83)

25. Whenever possible, I seek the most direct route through the maze of print in an attempt to beat the fact to the finish line. (83–84)

Now, to find your Reading Habit Score, do the following:
1. Total the check marks in each column here
2. Multiply each total as follows
3. Write your answer after multiplication here
4. Add up all of your answers (in line 3 above) and put the sum here _____%
(This is your Reading Habit Efficiency Score)

| X0 | X1 | X2 | X3 | X4 |

Compare your score with this scale:

90–100	Excellent reading habits
80–89	Good reading habits
70–79	Average reading habits
60–69	Below average reading habits
50–59	Poor reading habits
Below 50	Let's get on the ball!

What to do next: Note carefully the items checked in the first three columns.

Begin at once to strengthen each of these by *making it a habit* to practice them each time you face a page of print.

Newspaper Reading Interest Inventory
(See Discussion, Page 88)

Below is a list of features found in most large daily newspapers. Check the items in the list which you read regularly.

☐   1. Front-page news: national and international
☐   2. Local news
☐   3. Advertising: including major advertisements and the classified columns
☐   4. Business and financial news, including the stock reports
☐   5. Editorials
☐   6. Columnists
☐   7. Letters to the Editor
☐   8. Sports
☐   9. Fashions and homemaking news
☐ 10. News of science and scientific developments
☐ 11. Art news: (one or more) painting, sculpture, architecture
☐ 12. Crossword puzzles
☐ 13. Hobbies: (one or more) stamp and coin collecting, home improvement, gardening, photography
☐ 14. Radio and TV listening
☐ 15. Music: including records, FM, concerts, and music criticism
☐ 16. Education and school news
☐ 17. Literature: including book news and reviews, poetry
☐ 18. The theater, including the dance and choreography
☐ 19. Travel news
☐ 20. Guidance columns: advice to the lovelorn, the troubled, and the perplexed
☐ 21. Health news and medical advice
☐ 22. Obituaries
☐ 23. Religion and church news
☐ 24. Lost and found
☐ 25. Cartoons

SCORE; Number of items checked:_____. See page 88 for evaluation.

How Accurately Do You Read the News?

DIRECTIONS: With reference to the Centerville fire, you are asked as a witness in court whether, according to the account in the paper, the following statements were made categorically. Check the box in the appropriate column according to the way in which you would answer.

Statement	Was stated categorically	Was not stated categorically
1. The fire was at the plant of the Empire Tire and Rubber Company	☐	☐
2. The fire was of incendiary origin	☐	☐
3. The fire broke out after midnight	☐	☐
4. The fire was discovered by a night watchman	☐	☐
5. The damage amounted to $1,000,000	☐	☐
6. The flames raged out of control for four hours	☐	☐
7. The fire, a four-alarm blaze, brought fire-fighting equipment from all parts of the city	☐	☐
8. The fury of the fire was caused in part by exploding kegs of benzene stored in the processing division of the plant	☐	☐
9. The plant will be rebuilt	☐	☐
10. The president of the firm is E. B. Strongheart	☐	☐

Now, turn to the Answer Key, page 191, to check your answers. When you have found out how many items you answered correctly, record your score in the blank below.

Number of correct responses _____ × 10 = _____% Newspaper Reading Accuracy Index

How Large Is Your Financial-Page Vocabulary?

Directions: Place in the blank to the left of the item number in the left-hand column the letter indicating the expression in the right hand column which means the same or nearly the same as the word or phrase in the left-hand column.

_____	1. ad valorem	a.	a person or firm legally declared unable to pay its debts
_____	2. balance of trade	b.	an interest bearing certificate issued by a government or business promising to pay the holder a specified sum on a specified date.
_____	3. blue sky laws	c.	to pay off, to buy back, or convert into money
_____	4. gilt-edged	d.	one dollar
_____	5. ingot	e.	garnishment
_____	6. stock company	f.	difference between import-export value
_____	7. bank annuities	g.	corporate capital
_____	8. bullish	h.	British government bonds, consols.
_____	9. bankrupt	i.	puritanical prohibition of certain activities on Sunday
_____	10. interest	j.	a corporation whose capital is divided into shares
_____	11. bond	k.	a mass of metal poured into the form of a bar
_____	12. point	l.	stock in trade
_____	13. bearish	m.	money owed and so expressed as an entry on the left side of the ledger

_____ 14. portfolio

n. a list of stocks, bonds, and commercial paper owned by a bank or an individual

_____ 15. blue law

o. causing a rise in price on the stock market

_____ 16. trustee process

p. the highest quality or grade, said of bonds and securities

_____ 17. redeem

q. causing a lowering of prices on the stock exchange

_____ 18. maturity value

r. duties levied on imports accordingly to their invoiced value

_____ 19. inventory

s. regulation of stocks, bonds, etc. for the protection of the public

_____ 20. debit

t. the amount a note is worth on becoming due

u. money paid for the use of money

v. discount rate set by law

Check your answers for correctness. Turn to page 192. Enter your score, which will indicate your "financial page" vocabulary here:

Number correct _____ x 5 = _____ %

Code of Ethics of the International Reading Association

The Need for Establishing Standards

Until recently, reading was considered to be a rather simple process which should be learned in the early grades. We have now come to recognize it as a more complex act that develops within an individual throughout years of formal schooling and adult life. As a result the demand for trained personnel in reading at all levels has increased tremendously. With the demand high and the supply relatively short, the danger of unqualified persons attempting those tasks which only a trained reading specialist should undertake has become a very real one. One means of preventing such occurrences is by establishing minimum standards for the professional training of reading specialists. Part of the Code of Ethics of the International Reading Association is reprinted here because of so many practitioners, especially at the adult level, who purport to be "reading specialists" yet do not meet the standards of ethical practice in reading services as outlined by the Association.

The International Reading Association is the largest professional association of reading specialists in the world, and is truly international in scope and membership. Its members are concerned with the teaching of reading, committed to values which are the foundation of a democratic society, and have as their primary consideration the welfare of the public, the profession, and those individuals who may be preparing to teach reading or pursue graduate courses toward specialization in reading.

Ethical Standards in Reading Services

The following is a statement from the Code of Ethics of the International Reading Association:[1]

1. Reading specialists must possess suitable qualifications [i.e., a minimum of three years successful teaching and/or clinical experience; and a Master's Degree with a major emphasis in reading or its equivalent, or a Bachelor's Degree plus thirty hours of graduate courses in reading and related areas] for engaging in consulting, clinical, or remedial work. Unqualified persons should not engage in such activities, except under the direct supervision of one who is properly qualified. Professional intent and the welfare of the person seeking the services of the reading specialist should govern all consulting or clinical activities such as counseling, administering diagnostic tests, or providing remediation. It is the duty of the reading specialist to keep relationships with clients and interested persons on a professional level.

2. Information derived from consulting and/or clinical services should be regarded as confidential. Expressed consent of persons involved should be secured before releasing information to outside agencies.

3. Reading specialists should recognize the boundaries of their competence and should not offer services which fail to meet professional standards established by other disciplines. They should be free, however, to give assistance in other areas in which they are qualified.

4. Referral should be made to specialists in allied fields as needed. When such referral is made, pertinent informa-

[1] Copies of the Code of Ethics may be secured by writing to the Professional Standards and Ethics Committee, International Reading Association, Box 695, Newark, Delaware 19711.

tion should be made available to consulting specialists.

5. Reading clinics and/or reading specialists offering professional services should refrain from guaranteeing easy solutions or favorable outcomes as a result of their work, and their advertising should be consistent with that of allied professions. They should not accept for remediation any persons who are unlikely to benefit from their instruction, and they should work to accomplish the greatest possible improvement in the shortest time. Fees, if charged, should be agreed on in advance and should be charged in accordance with an established set of rates commensurate with that of the other professions.

Let the Buyer Be Wary[2]

A wide variety of services, devices and training materials which purport to produce the improvement of reading skills is currently being offered to the general public. In some instances, the advertising accompanying these materials approaches sensationalism, exaggeration and even misrepresentation, when judged with regard to the limits of present professional knowledge.

To aid the prospective user of reading improvement devices and services, the International Reading Association offers the following cautions:

1. Statements of possible benefits from reading improvement services should be characterized by modesty and due caution for the limits of professional skills which do not encompass cure-all powers.

2. The possible causes of inadequate or poor reading skills are many. There is no single treatment or approach known which will effectively correct all possible causes of difficulty.

3. No ethical person who is a professional in the area of

[2] Resolution adopted by the Delegates Assembly at the Tenth Annual Convention of the International Reading Association.

reading improvement can or should guarantee marked improvement of skills for all users of his services.

4. Distributors of reading devices or materials have an ethical obligation to submit their products to fair scientific trials before marketing, and to make the data of these evaluations available to all prospective purchasers.

Answer key

How Alert Are You?

   1. d;   2. d,g;   3. d;   4. c.

How Accurately Do You Recall?

   1. Ralph Smallwood.   2. HI-1 4202 (If you were alert you would have noticed how easily this lent itself to a formula: "Call me, highland one, for to (g)o, too.")   3. (a) Resolve to remember. (b) Rescue the fact frequently. (c) Find a formula. (Did you notice a kind of formula here also: First 2 r's (Resolve to remember); then 1 r, 2 f's; then 2 f's).   4. A good beginning is half the journey. 5. Victims in a quicksand.   6. Ingenuity.

How Many F's Did You Find?

   There are six F's in the sentence. The average reader finds only three of them. This is poor in terms of perceptual achievement. Seeing four is fair; five is good; six, excellent.

How Large Is Your Word-Hoard?

1. c	6. d	11. e	16. b	21. a
2. d	7. c	12. a	17. b	22. b
3. b	8. e	13. a	18. a	23. d
4. a	9. b	14. d	19. b	24. d
5. c	10. c	15. a	20. c	25. c

How Well Do You Sense Structure?

The correct structural pattern is III.

A. General discussion of good reading and the qualities a good reader possesses

B. Personal qualities you need to read well
1. Alertness
2. Recall
a. Resolve to remember
b. Rescue the fact frequently
c. Find a formula
3. Vision and perception
4. Word-Hoard
5. Structure sense

C. Increasing speed of reading (a summarizing section)

How Keen Is Your Sense of Acuteness and Awareness in Reading Paragraphs?

NOT EVERYTHING IS A PARAGRAPH THAT LOOKS LIKE ONE

A   [1] Appearances are deceptive. [2] ∧ _Because_ Authors are whimsical.
For example
[3] ∧ Not everything *is* a paragraph that looks like one.

B   [1] The reader must always be in command. [2] In facing a
for example
page of print, ∧ nothing replaces the agile, active, inquiring, analyzing mind of a reader who knows exactly what the author is saying because that reader knows exactly what the author is doing with the thought and precisely what is transpiring upon the page.

C   ([1] *Incidentally, have you been in command?* [2] ∧ _Or_ *Has the somewhat complex structure of the thought in the last two paragraphs eluded you?* [3] *At the close of this section you will have an opportunity to test your "command status," so that you will want to keep alert from here on.* [4] *Watch for read-ing booby traps.*)

D   [1] Indentations in the left margin of print usually signal
the beginning of a new thought. [2] $\underset{\wedge}{\overset{But}{}}$ This is not always true.
[3] It may mean $\underset{\wedge}{\overset{for\ example}{}}$ that the author is merely providing "reader relief."

E   [1] $\underset{\wedge}{\overset{Because}{}}$ Great blocks of print are depressing to many readers.
[2] They see them $\underset{\wedge}{\overset{therefore}{}}$ as ponderous and forbidding. [3] $\underset{\wedge}{\overset{And,\ furthermore}{}}$ Authors know
this. [4] They sometimes break up a longer discussion $\underset{\wedge}{\overset{therefore}{}}$ into sub-
discussions—as $\underset{\wedge}{\overset{for\ example}{}}$ we have been doing in this chapter with this
rather extended discussion of the paragraph—or perhaps an
extended paragraph into subparagraphs.

F   [1] Reasons $\underset{\wedge}{\overset{for\ example}{}}$ may be detached from the facts which they logically justify. [2] $\underset{\wedge}{\overset{Again}{}}$ Examples may be separated by paragraph
division from the principles which they illustrate. [3] Logically
$\underset{\wedge}{\overset{however}{}}$ these should be in the same prose package with the material with which they are inseparably linked. [4] $\underset{\wedge}{\overset{But}{}}$ This may form
inordinately long discussions and paragraph structures which,
because of their very length, may have adverse psychological
effects on the reader.

G   [1] It is psychologically advantageous $\underset{\wedge}{\overset{for\ instance}{}}$ occasionally to separate integrally connected parts of a discussion, $\underset{\wedge}{\overset{although}{}}$ to do so
places a greater burden upon your reading skill and ability,
your acuteness and sense of awareness of what is happening
on the page.

II. The order of the sentences should be 1,3,2. The first sentence is the main idea (topic) sentence, and should come first. Next, an example, illustrating the main idea, follows. Finally, the reason for the first two sentences is given. (The reason why the example is true)

III. Paragraphs E and F should be incorporated. Paragraph F is a fragmentary paragraph that logically is a part of paragraph E, because it presents an example of the last sentence in paragraph E.

IV. A, B, (C), D   A should be encircled.
     E, F, G   E should be encircled.
Editorial captions might be: Appearances Are Deceptive.
                               Blocks of Print Are Depressing.

Dots and Dashes That Help You Read Better

The sentence is punctuated so that it may be read for meaning—with commas and semicolons inserted where pauses of lesser or greater duration should occur. The placement of the punctuation marks does not necessarily follow the conventional rules for punctuation but is for functional assistance in reading only. Try reading the sentence like this:

That, that is, is; that is, is that that is; but that, that is not, is not that, that is.

DIDYOUEVERSEEABUNDANCEONTHETABLE

You cannot possibly tell what this sentence says, because the meaning depends upon the grouping of letters and the separation of group from group. One way of grouping and separating the letters results in this sentence:

Did you ever see a bun dance on the table?

Another grouping and separation of the respective groups results in this:

Did you ever see abundance on the table?

Who knows precisely what it says?

How Large Is Your Word-Hoard—Now?

1. e	5. d	9. b	13. c	17. a
2. d	6. c	10. a	14. e	18. d
3. b	7. b	11. c	15. a	19. b
4. d	8. c	12. a	16. e	20. d

Punctuation Makes All the Difference

1. The sign should have been punctuated as follows:

PRIVATE?
NO! SWIMMING
ALLOWED

The answers to the other questions follow: 2. (b), 3. (a), 4. (a), 5. (b), 6. (a), 7. (a), 8. (b), 9. (a), 10. (b).

How Accurately Do You Read the News?

This test is to determine whether you are a careful, critical reader of the newspaper. If you read carefully and critically you will have noted the word *categorically* in the test. Categorically means unconditionally, unqualifiedly, absolutely, positively, explicitly. Below is a tabulation of the answers and the supporting reasons.

In Statement:	*You should have checked the —*	*For the following reason:*
1.	First column	This was a fact as stated in the news report.
2.	Second column	The article did *not* say categorically that the fire was of incendiary origin, but that it was *reported* to have been of incendiary origin.
3.	Second column	The fire *was discovered* after midnight. It may have broken out (started) much earlier.

4.	Second column	Fire Chief Smith *reported* that a night watchman discovered the blaze; the report may have been incorrect.
5.	Second column	The $1,000,000 is merely an *estimate*.
6.	First column	This was a fact stated in the news report.
7.	First column	This was a fact stated in the news report.
8.	Second column	The article merely *speculates* that the fury of the fire may have been due to benzene: "*apparently* fed by quantities of benzene . . . ." The article does not even say the benzene was in kegs.
9.	Second column	This is merely E. B. Strongheart's *opinion;* you cannot accept it as fact.
10.	First column	This was a fact as stated in the news report.

To score your test: Give each correct answer ten points. Record your score on the chart on page 182.

How Large Is Your Financial-Page Vocabulary?

1. r	5. k	9. a	13. q	17. c
2. f	6. j	10. u	14. n	18. t
3. s	7. h	11. b	15. i	19. l
4. p	8. o	12. d	16. e	20. m

Index

About Paul D. Leedy

A nationally known pioneer in the field of adult reading, Dr. Paul D. Leedy has taught at the Reading Institute, New York University, and at Dickinson College, Fairleigh Dickinson University, and the University of Colorado. He is currently Professor of Education at The American University in Washington, D.C. Dr. Leedy is also the author of *Reading Improvement for Adults* and *Read with Speed and Precision,* both published by McGraw-Hill, and a McGraw-Hill paperback reprint, *Improve Your Reading.*

1 *This column contains the reading needs expressed by most adults*

1. What does it take to read well?
   Do I have the requirements?

2. How does a skilled reader handle a page of print?

3. How can I improve my rate of reading?

4. What should I know about reading a paragraph?

5. How can punctuation help me to read better?

6. How can I improve my vocabulary?

7. Some people take a book and, in a few minutes tell you all about it. How do they do this?

8. What is the best way to read a newspaper?

9. How does one read editorials, the financial page, and the funnies?

10. Some people pick up every inference, every nuance of meaning in reading. How do they do this?

11. How can I clear my desk and keep it clear?

12. Some people are sensitive to the beauty of language. How can I acquire this awareness?

13. Some people sense the structure of writing quickly. How do they do it?

14. How can I plan an intelligent course of action to improve my reading?

15. How well formed are my reading habits?